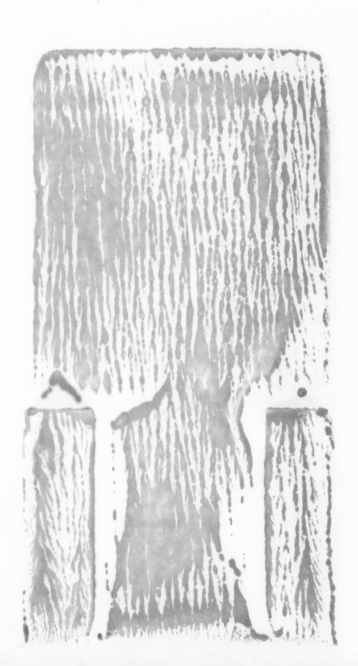

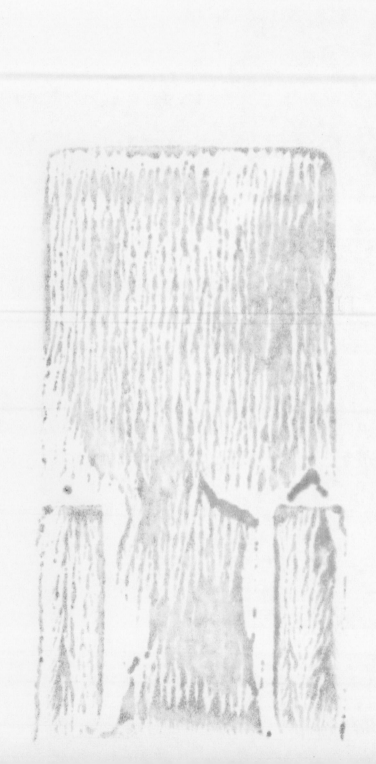

# THE CHAUCER CANON

*SKEAT*

¶ Jack vp Lande
Compyled by the
famous Geoffrey
Chaucer.

Ezechielis. xiii.
¶ Wo be vnto you that
dishonour me to me peo
ple for an handful of bar
lye & for a pece of bread.

Cum priuilegio
Regali.

TITLE-PAGE TO JACK UPLAND

ABOUT A.D. 1536

# THE CHAUCER CANON

WITH A DISCUSSION OF THE

WORKS ASSOCIATED WITH THE NAME

OF

## GEOFFREY CHAUCER

BY THE

## REV. WALTER W. SKEAT

LITT.D., D.C.L., LL.D., PH.D.

*Elrington and Bosworth Professor of Anglo-Saxon, and
Fellow of Christ's College, Cambridge*

'Dare not to match thy pype with Tityrus his style'
SPENSER, *Shep. Kal. Epilogue*

## HASKELL HOUSE
### Publishers of Scholarly Books
NEW YORK
### 1965

First Published 1900

**HASKELL HOUSE PUBLISHERS** Ltd.
*Publishers of Scarce Scholarly Books*
280 LAFAYETTE STREET
NEW YORK, N. Y. 10012

Library of Congress Catalog Card Number: 68–817

Haskell House Catalogue Item # 623

# PREFACE

THE subject of the present volume is an examination of the Chaucer Canon. All the pieces that have been at any time associated with his name are here considered; and various tests are given whereby his genuine works can be distinguished from the rest.

Much that is here said is necessarily repeated from what I have already advanced in my six-volume edition of Chaucer and in the supplementary volume entitled Chaucerian Pieces; but I have also taken the opportunity, whilst collecting many scattered observations that have been previously made, of introducing a few new suggestions and arguments. In particular, the account here given of the striking parallel between Chaucer's grammatical usages and the regular employment of various grammatical suffixes in the unassailable text of the Ormulum is, to the best of my belief, wholly new, and adds much firmness and certainty to the whole argument. It is true that Tyrwhitt (in note 69 to his Essay on Chaucer's Language) long ago pointed out the value of 'the practice of Orm, the most authentic metrical composer that we have in our antient language,' but he did not give any detailed account of the conclusions to be drawn from it.

The argument which I adduce is briefly this. The extreme regularity of the metre of the Ormulum enables us to deduce with certainty the circumstances under which grammatical inflexions are employed in it. Precisely similar inflexions occur in the genuine works of Chaucer, but not (speaking generally) in works which have erroneously been connected with his name.

Further, the genuine works, and these only, satisfy various rime-tests which are duly explained, and are all deducible from the Canterbury Tales; and in this way the true Chaucer Canon can be established.

A recent article by Dr. Koch, which appeared in the Englische Studien after the main part of the present work had been printed, has suggested the addition of the 'Note on Chapter VI,' printed at p. 149.

The results here arrived at have been compared with those given in Prof. Lounsbury's 'Chaucer Studies,' from which they do not materially differ. Writing in 1892, Prof. Lounsbury was disposed to claim for Chaucer the whole of the existing English translation of the Romaunt of the Rose; but later investigations have shown that this view is no longer tenable.

An Appendix is subjoined, containing a complete List of Chaucer's Works, a List of Authorities for the same, and a Chronological List of all works associated with Chaucer, in the exact order of their publication.

I am indebted to Professor Hales for kindly perusing the proof sheets, though he is in no way responsible for their contents.

W. W. S.

# TABLE OF CONTENTS

# ERRATA

P. 46, l. 11.   For *Russy-e*, 1 ; read *Russy-e*, 9 ;
P. 53, l. 3 from foot.   For *tombestéres* read *tombestères*

# THE CHAUCER CANON

## CHAPTER I

### INTRODUCTION

**1.** THE object of this treatise is to explain clearly the chief peculiarities of Chaucer's grammar and versification. If these are once exactly and accurately comprehended, it becomes easy, even for a reader who has had no previous training, to distinguish his genuine poems from those that have been attributed to him, at various times, by the carelessness or wantonness of editors and critics. In this way the true Canon of Chaucer's Works can be compiled with ease and certainty, and can no longer be controverted, in the future, except by such as deny the existence of arguments which it is inconvenient to understand.

**2.** Owing to the prevalence of much ignorance on this subject, which at one time was inevitable, but is now (thanks to the Chaucer Society and its founder) no longer necessary and will one day be discreditable, a large number of misrepresentations, misconceptions, and—to be plain—downright falsehoods have been printed and circulated in former years [1]. Some of these will be noticed as occasion arises; others will be corrected in the process of investigation. For this reason, I shall begin at the beginning, with but

---

[1] See, for example, Stowe's treatment of the date of The Craft of Lovers, discussed in § 105 below.

*one* postulate ; and this is one that will readily be granted, if it be only for the convenience of argument.

**3. Chaucer the author of the Canterbury Tales.** Let it be granted that the name of the author of the Canterbury Tales was Geoffrey Chaucer. It is worth saying that this fact, universally admitted and accepted, is expressly asserted in the MSS. Thus in the colophon of the celebrated Ellesmere MS. we have :—'Here is ended the book of the Tales of Caunterbury, compiled by Geffrey Chaucer, of whos soule Iesu Crist have mercy.' Many of the MSS. are imperfect at the end; but a similar ascription is found in the Petworth MS. and in Harl. 1758. The celebrated MS. Harl. 7334 has no colophon, but the last paragraph is headed 'Preces de Chauceres,' where the Ellesmere MS. has :—'Here taketh the makere of this book his leve.' In the prologue to Sir Thopas MS. E. has the rubric:—'Bihoold the murye wordes of the Hoost to Chaucer'; and the Tale itself is headed 'Heere bigynneth Chaucers Tale of Thopas.' When the host interrupts it, we find :—'Heere the Hoost stynteth Chaucer of his Tale of Thopas.' The tale of Melibeus is headed:— 'Heere bigynneth Chaucers Tale of Melibee'; and there is a similar note at the end of the same. But the most important reference is in The Man of Lawes Prologue, B 47, where Chaucer first of all mentions himself by name in the third person, and immediately afterwards proceeds to allude to two more of his own works, viz. the poem of 'Ceys and Alcion,' preserved in The Book of the Duchess, and the very important poem usually known as The Legend of Good Women.

**4.** The Canterbury Tales constitute a poem of such extent that it amply suffices as a store-house whence all the more important peculiarities of the poet's grammar and versification can be safely deduced ; and when we are once in possession of these, it becomes an easy matter to see

whether such peculiarities are equally well represented in
such poems as are known to be his *from external evidence.*
It is not prejudging the enquiry to say that such will be
found to be the case ; whereas it will further be found that—
except in a very few instances, which must be especially considered—the works which have only been *casually* associated
with his name exhibit such wide differences from the
methods which he can be proved to have used as to pre-
clude all possibility of his having had any share in them.

**5.** The mere fact that Chaucer wrote the Canterbury
Tales enables us at once to clear out of the way two of the
notions that have, at various times, been put forward by
way of argument. The first of these is that Chaucer
was not very particular as to his grammar or his rimes in
his earlier years, but afterwards became more accurate ;
a theory in itself just the reverse of what would be probable, when we remember that the movement in linguistic
usage was, at this period, in the direction of simplification
and of decrease in the use of inflexions. The second is,
that Chaucer employed provincialisms in his earlier days
which he afterwards lost ; a supposition purely gratuitous.
However, we know that The Canterbury Tales consist of
a collection of things new and old, and we have it on the
authority of the author himself that the ' Lyf of seint
Cecyle,' which afterwards became 'The Seconde Nunnes
Tale,' was written before the Legend of Good Women,
and it has even been conjectured to have been amongst
the earliest of his works. Yet all the Tales agree as to
grammatical usage, dialect[1], and peculiarities of rime ; and
we need not make any allowances on the score of chrono-
logy. The general results are, linguistically, much the
same as if all the Tales had been written in the same year.

---

[1] Excepting, of course, the famous passage in the Reves Tale,
where the Northern dialect is purposely introduced, with a fair
degree of accuracy.

In the later tales, the style is easier, and the vocabulary richer; but the grammar remains unaltered.

**6.** Some of those who persist in attributing to Chaucer certain works with which he had nothing to do are naturally interested in minimising the number and force of the arguments that militate against their genuineness. It is pretended that it is merely a question of a few abnormal rimes, and other similar indications which are, quite wrongly, assumed to be of small moment[1]. But the fact is that, even if all the rimes in the spurious poems were strictly correct, which is very far from being the case, we should still have to consider the much more momentous questions of linguistic and grammatical usage. Our first enquiries should, accordingly, be turned in this direction; for if we can once assure ourselves as to what were the precise peculiarities of grammar which Chaucer employed, we can soon detect, with ease and certainty, the grievous sins against his standards which are so conspicuous in pieces that really belong to a later century. These are points which a literary critic is very glad to try to set aside; but they happen to be very numerous and unmistakeably clear, when once collected and explained; and most uncompromisingly fatal, in many instances, to ingenious but impossible theories as to the authorship of such pieces. It would have been somewhat easy for a writer in the fifteenth century to observe Chaucer's rimes, if he wished his piece to be mistaken for one written by the master, and it would have been still more easy to copy his language and turns of phrase; but there was one thing which the fifteenth-century writer never achieved, and that was a precise knowledge of the *grammar* of the preceding

---

[1] Even a single false rime may be fatal, such as *storm* and *corn* in Rom. Rose, 4343. We are asked if we should apply a like rule to Tennyson, to which I answer—yes! Was Tennyson capable of riming *storm* with *corn*?

century. Indeed, it may be doubted whether, towards the
middle of the century, there were any readers left who
knew how to scan Chaucer's lines properly; and, in the
sixteenth century, all such knowledge had so utterly died
out that the editors of the black-letter editions made no
attempt to reduce the lines to order, but left them in a
state of utter ruggedness whenever they happened not to
see their way to the true lilt of the line. Thus, in Stowe's
edition of 1561, we find, near the beginning of the Prologue, such lines as these :—

> 'The drought of Marche had perced[1] the rote';   2
> 'Espired[2] hath[3] euery holte and heth';   6
> 'The tendre croppes, and the yong[4] sonne';   7
> 'And palmers[5] to seken straunge strondes';   13
> 'Redie to go[6] in my pilgrimage';   21

By observing a few such lines, we at once see that
Dryden, who only knew Chaucer from editions of this
character, was perfectly justified in his apparently severe
remarks :—'The verse of Chaucer, I confess, is not har-
monious to us. . . It were an easy matter to produce some
thousands of his verses, which are lame for want of half
a foot, and sometimes a whole one,' incautiously adding—
'and which no pronunciation can make otherwise.' The
last remark is not of general application ; for though it is
applicable to four of the five verses quoted above, it is
untrue with regard to line 7. For though it is the case that,
in modern English, we should justly brand as detestable
such a line as—'The tender crops, and the young sun '—
it becomes beautifully melodious when we learn that the
plural of *crop*, in Chaucerian English, assumed the dissyllabic form *cropp-ès*, while the definite form of the adjective *young*, necessitated by the use of the definite article

---

[1] Here *to* is omitted.   [2] Error for *Enspired.*   [3] Here *in* is
omitted.   [4] Read *yong-e* (dissyllabic).   [5] Here *for* is omitted.
[6] For *go* read *wenden.*

preceding it, likewise assumed the dissyllabic form *yong-è*. The true form is, accordingly, the following :—

  'The tendre croppès, and the yongè sonnè.'

And this is a perfect line, even when some of the words are mispronounced by giving the vowels their present modern values.

**7.** This simple example shews the vital importance of understanding Chaucer's grammar, if we are to make anything at all of scanning his lines. It is worth saying here that, as a matter of fact, Chaucer's pronunciation can be shown, by comparison with that of other authors, to be of an archaic rather than of a progressive character. It is that of the London English of the fourteenth century, and tends much more to conformity with that of the preceding thirteenth century than with that of the succeeding fifteenth. This is a point which has by no means been clearly brought out by critics, but it will be found to be true ; and the remembrance of the fact will be found to be helpful. The extent to which this is really the case will appear ere long.

**8.** It is well to consider for a moment whether we can depend on the integrity of the text. Fortunately, we have, in the Ellesmere MS. of the Canterbury Tales, an excellent authority that seldom fails, and one that from a phonetic point of view may be characterised as being very well spelt. The text of the Tales is admirably safe, when compared, for example, with the text of Shakespeare. It is very rarely that any restoration or emendation becomes necessary ; and even then, we have such fair authorities as the Hengwrt, the Cambridge, the Corpus, and (in some cases) the Harleian manuscripts. It is hardly too much to say that we sometimes meet with many hundred consecutive lines in which there can be no hesitation whatever as to what the real reading must be.

For all this, it might be urged by such as desire to raise objections, that it is somewhat illogical to deduce the rules for scansion from the very text which it may be occasionally desirable to amend.   The answer is ready, viz. that it is perfectly logical to deduce rules from the thousands of lines which are beyond suspicion, and to apply them to the cases where difficulties seem to arise.   Nevertheless, in order to cut away even this pretence of complaint, I shall show how all the chief rules of Chaucer's grammar can be deduced from the text of the older and metrically perfect poem entitled the Ormulum, the scansion of which admits of no two opinions.   When rules have been obtained from this irrefragable authority, it will be easy to show how they can be applied to the scansion of Chaucer ; and this will place the argument beyond the possibility of error.

**9.** In that remarkable poem, belonging to the first quarter of the thirteenth century, we possess a document above suspicion, which for all purposes of metre is of the highest value.   Its authority cannot be contested, because it is an autograph copy written in a purely phonetic notation by an author who paid a most remarkable attention to pronunciation and to points of grammar.   Besides this, it so happens that his metre is of a most uncompromising regularity, admitting of no variation.   So much is this the case that the reader is apt to grow weary at last of its merciless monotony, and is in a humour to pardon the author at once, if he would only consent to break out into some wild exhibition of irregularity ; but of this he feels that there is no hope.   Every line, without exception [1], contains fifteen syllables, neither more nor less, and is capable of being divided into two nearly equal parts.   The former of these contains eight syllables exactly, and the latter contains seven ; and this is continued for thousands and

---

[1] Of course we must not count in such syllables as are obviously elided.

thousands of consecutive lines, leaving no doubt at all as to the author's usage. The general effect of Ormin's line is easily exemplified by comparison with the first two lines of Campbell's poem entitled 'Lord Ullin's daughter' :—

> 'A chieftain, to the Highlands bound,
>   Cries, "Boatman, do not tarry!"'

The dialect of the Ormulum is more purely East Midland than that of Chaucer, being free from admixture of Southern forms; it is also, of course, more archaic. Still there is sufficient similarity for our present investigation. The peculiar spelling is excellent for phonetic purposes, but somewhat bizarre and puzzling to the general reader. I shall therefore transliterate it into Chaucerian spelling, which can be done with perfect ease and certainty by any one who understands the pronunciation of the two poems. The convenience of the transliteration is obvious; and the original is perfectly accessible to the scholar[1]. I select the first 156 lines of the Prologue, as being sufficient. In making the transliteration, I may observe that I use *y* to represent *ī*, the sound of *ee* in *ween*, in order to distinguish it from *i*, the sound of *i* in *win*. I use *ee* and *oo* to denote long vowels in words like *yeer* (year), *book* (book) that terminate with a consonant; also *ou* or *ow* (if final), as in the Chaucer MSS., to denote the long *ū* in *hūs*, a house, riming with mod. E. *goose*. In the original such words as *that* and *theer* (there) are invariably altered to *tat* and *teer* when the preceding word ends in *d* or *t*; a peculiarity which, for our purpose, it is needless to preserve. The only point, in fact, that requires careful observation is the varying value of the final *-e*, which always forms a syllable of the verse unless it be elided before a vowel, and at the same time does duty as an important grammatical in-

---

[1] A sufficient specimen is given in Morris, Specimens of Early English, Part I. pp. 40–63.

flexion in many ways.   In order to present the results more
clearly, the inflexions *-en, -es, -e,* are marked off by the use
of a hyphen, and every elided final *-e* is printed in italics.

### 10. Introduction to the Ormulum.

Now, brother Walter, brother myn
>   After the flesh-es kynd-e;
And brother myn in Cristendoom
>   Through fullought and through trouth-e;
And brother myn in Godd-es hous                             5
>   Yet on the thridd-e wys-e,
Through that wit hav-en tak-en bo
>   Oon reghel-book to folw-en,
Under canunk-es hood and lyf
>   So som Saint Austin sett-e;                            10
I hav-e doon so som thou bad
>   And forth-ed thee thyn will-e,
I hav-e wend intíl Englísh
>   Gospell-es holy lor-e,
After that litel wit that me                               15
>   Myn Drighten hav-eth len-ed.
Thou thoughtest that it might-e wel
>   To mikel fram-e turn-en,
If English folk, for lov*e* of Crist,
>   It wold-e yern-e lern-en,                              20
And folw-en it, and fill-en it
>   With thought, with word, with ded-e.
And forthy yerndest thou that I
>   This werk thee shold-e werk-en,

---

2. *kynde,* nature.          4. *fullought,* baptism.          6. Yet in the
third way.          7. *wit,* we two (dual) ; *bo,* both.          8. One rule-
book to follow.          9. *canunkes hood,* canon's hood.          10, 11. *So
som,* so as. just as.          12. And furthered for thee thy will.          13.
*wend,* turned.          16. My Lord hath lent (me).          18. *frame,*
profit.          20. *yerne,* eagerly.          21. *fillen,* fulfil, practise.          23.
And therefore thou desiredst.

And I it hav-e forth-ed thee,                               25
   But al through Crist-es help-e ;
And unc birth both-e thank-en Crist
   That it is broght to end-e.
I hav-e samn-ed on this book
   The gospell-es neigh all-e,                    30
That sind-en in the mess-e-book
   In al the yeer at mess-e.
And ay aftér the gospel stant
   That that the gospel meneth,
That man birth spell-en to the folk                        35
   Of their-e sowl-e ned-e ;
And yet ther-tek-en mor*e* inogh
   Thou shalt ther-onn-e find-en
Of that that Crist-es holy theed
   Birth trow-en wel and folw-en.                 40
I hav-e sét heer, in this book,
   Among gospéll-es word-es,
Al through my-selv-en, many word
   The rym-e so to fill-en ;
But thou shalt find-en that my word,                       45
   Aywher ther it is ek-ed,
May help-en tho that red-en it
   To seen and t'understand-en
Al this the better how theym birth
   The gospel understand-en ;                     50
And fórthy trow*e* I that thee birth
   Wel thol-en myn-e word-es

---

25. And I have advanced it for thee.   27. And it behoves us-two (*dual*) both.   29. *samned*, collected.   31. *sinden*, are ; *messebook*, mass-book.   33. *ay*, always ; *stant*, stands. 35. That one ought to explain.   37. *ther-teken*, moreover. 39. *theed*, people.   40. Ought to believe well.   46. Everywhere where it is added.   47. *tho*, those.   49. how it behoves them.   51. *forthy*, therefore ; *thee birth*, it behoves thee. 52. *tholen*, suffer.

Aywher ther thou shalt fynd-en hem
Among gospéll-es word-es.
For who-so moot to lew-ed folk　　　　55
Loor-spell of gospel tell-en,
He moot wel ek-en many word
Among gospéll-es word-es.
And I ne might-e not my vers
Ay with gospéll-es word-es　　　　60
Wel fill-en al; and al forthy
Sholde I wel oft-e ned-e
Among gospéll-es word-es doon
My word, my vers to fill-en.
And thee biteche I of this book,　　　65
Heigh wik-en as it semeth,
Al to through-sek-en ech a vers
And 'to through-lok-en oft-e,
That úpon al this book ne be
No word geyn Cristes lor-e,　　　　70
No word that swyth-e wel ne be
To trow-en and to folw-en.
Wit shull-en tred-en under foot
And al thwert-out forwerp-en
The doom of al that loth-e flok　　　75
That is through nith forblend-ed,
That tēl-eth that to lov-en is
Through nithful modiness-e.
They shull-en let-en heth-e-ly
Of unker swink, leef brother;　　　80

55. *lewed folk*, the laity.　　56. *Loor-spell*, teaching.　　57. *eken*, add.　　62. *nede*, of necessity.　　65. And I charge thee, as to this book.　　66. Great duty as it seems (to be).　　70. *geyn*, contrary to.　　71. *swythe*, very, quite.　　73. We-two ought. 74. And all wholly cast out.　　75. *lothe*, hostile.　　76. That is blinded by envy.　　77. *teleth*, vilifies ; *that to loven is*, that which is praiseworthy.　　78. envious pride.　　79. They will be sure to think scornfully.　　80. Of the work of us-two (*dual*).

And al they shull-en tak-en it
    On unnit and on idel;
But not through skil, but al through nith,
    And al through theyr-e sinn-e.
And unk birth bidd-en God that he      85
    Forgive hem hir-e sinn-e;
And unk birth both-e lov-en God
    Of that it was begunn-en,
And thank-en God that it is broght
    To end-e, through his help-e;      90
For it may help-en all-e tho
    That blith-e-ly it her-en,
And lov-en it, and folw-en it
    With thoght, with word, with ded-e.
And who-so wil-en shal this book      95
    Eft other syth-e wryt-en,
Him bidde I that he't wryt-e right
    So som this book him tech-eth
Al thwert-out after that it is
    Upon this first-e bisn-e,      100
With all such ryme as heer is set,
    With al so fel-e word-es;
And that he lok-e wel that he
    Oon book-staf wryt-e twy-es
Aywher ther it upon this book      105
    Is writ-en on that wys-e.
Loke he wel that he't wryt-e so,
    For he ne may not ell-es

82. As being useless and vain. 83. *skil*, reason; *nith*, envy. 85. And it behoves us-two to pray. 86. *hire*, their. 87. *loven*, praise. 95. *wilen shal*, shall desire. 96. To write again, on another occasion. 97. I pray him; *he't*, he it. 98. *So som*, even as. 99. All throughout according as. 100. *bisne*, copy. 102. With just so many words. 103. *loke wel*, pay great heed. 104. Write one letter twice. 105. Wherever it. 107. *he't*, he it. 108. *elles*, otherwise.

In English wryt-en right the word,
  That wit*e* he wel to soth-e.        110
And if man wil-e wit-en why
  I hav-e doon this ded-e,
Why I to English hav-e wend
  Gospéll-es holy lor-e;
I hav*e* it doon forthy that al       115
  Cristen-e folk-es berghles
Is long upon that oon, that they
  Gospéll-es holy lor-e
With full-e might-e folw-e right
  Through thoght, through word, through ded-e. 120
For al that evr*e* on erth is need
  Cristen-e folk to folw-en
In trouth*e*, in ded*e*, al tech-eth hem
  Gospéll-es holy lor-e.
And fórthy who-so lern-eth it      125
  And folw-eth it with ded-e,
He shal on end-e worthy been
  Through God to worth-en borw-en.
And therfor*e* hav*e* I turn-ed it
  Intil Englísh-e spech-e,      130
For that I wold-e blyth-e-ly
  That al Englísh-e led-e
With er-e shold-e list-en it,
  With hert-e shold*e* it trow-en,
With tung-e shold-e spell-en it,     135

110. Let him know that well, for a truth.    111. And if one
desires to know why.    113. *wend,* turned.    115. *forthy,*
because.    116. (all) the salvation of Christian people.    117.
Depends on that one (thing).    119. With all their power may
follow (what is) right.    121. For everything that it is ever
necessary in this world.    122. (For) Christian people to perform.
125. And therefore.    127. *on ende,* at last.    128. To be saved
by God.    132. *lede,* folks.    133. *ere,* ear.    134. *trowen,*
believe.

With ded-e sholde it folw-en,
To winn-en under Cristendoom
At God sooth sowl-e berghles.
And if they wil-en her-en it,
  And folw-en it with ded-e,                              140
I have hem holp-en, under Crist,
  To winn-en theyr-e berghles.
And I shal hav-en for my swink
  Good loon at God on end-e,
If that I, for the love of God                              145
  And for the mede of hev'n-e,
Hem have it into English wend
  For theyr-e sowl-e ned-e.
And if they al forwerp-en it,
  It turn-eth hem to sinn-e,                              150
And I shal hav-en addl-ed me
  The lōverd Crist-es or-e,
Through that I have hem wroght this book
  To theyr-e sowl-e ned-e,
Thogh that they al forwerp-en it                              155
  Through theyr-e modiness-e.

**11.** The above extract does not quite exhaust the grammatical uses of the final *-en* and *-e*, but it is sufficient to give some of the chief rules, and it clearly establishes the principle, viz. that, *without* an accurate knowledge of Middle-English grammar, no one can be in a position to consider the scansion of Chaucer's verse, or is competent to consider questions regarding the true canon of his works.

---

13⁸. At (the hands of) God true salvation of soul.      139. *wilen*, desire.      141. *holpen*, helped.      142. To win their salvation. 143. *swink*, toil.      144. Good reward from God at last.      147. *wend*, turned.      149. *forwerpen*, reject.      150. *hem*, to them, for them.      151. *addled*, earned (for myself).      152. The grace of the Lord Christ.      155. *forwerpen*, reject.      156. *modinesse*, pride.

Obvious as this may be, it is continually neglected in practice; and few things are more common, or perhaps *were* more common, than to find confident opinions pronounced by men who have no right to be heard, because they neither know the grammatical facts nor the true pronunciation of the words. A knowledge of the latter is not absolutely necessary, but is obviously of great assistance, and should at any rate be acquired by all who presume to teach. Those who do not aspire to instruct others can, of course, do as they please. I now proceed to tabulate some of the more important facts which the above extract infallibly teaches us.

**12. Final *-en* in the Ormulum.** The following examples of final *-en* may be noted. The reference, in every case, is to the numbering of the lines in the above extract.

(*a*) Final *-en* marks the use of *the infinitive mood.* Exx. *turn-en*, 18; *lern-en*, 20; *folw-en*, 21; *fill-en*, 21; *werk-en*, 24; *thank-en*, 27; *spell-en*, 35; *find-en*, 38; &c. In Chaucer, this final *-en* is often reduced to *-e*; but the *-e* constitutes a separate syllable.

(*b*) Final *-en* marks the use of *the gerund*, which is known by the occurrence of *to* before it. Exx. *to folw-en*, 8, 72, 122; *to lov-en*, 77; *To winn-en*, 137. In Chaucer, this final *-en* is sometimes reduced to *-e* (a separate syllable), but is seldom elided. As the gerund was expressive of purpose, it seems to have been more emphatic, and the termination was even more important than in the preceding case.

(*c*) Final *-en* marks the *past participle of a strong verb*; i. e. of verbs like our *sing* (pt. t. *sang*, pp. *sung*), in the conjugation of which *a change of the vowel* is a marked feature, whilst, at the same time, the said pp. does *not* end in *-ed*, *-d*, or *-t* (as in *sough-t* from *seek* .

Exx. *tak-en*, 7; *begunn-en*, 88; *writ-en* (mod. E. *written*), 106; *borw-en*, 128; *holp-en*, 141. This termination can still be traced in modern English, as in *taken, written.*   In Chaucer, this *-en* is often reduced to *-e.*

(*d*) Final *-en* marks the use of *the plural of a verbal tense,* whether in *the present indicative or subjunctive,* or (chiefly in the case of strong verbs) in *the past tense.*   In the above extracts, the examples happen to refer to the present tense.   Exx.  *sind-en,*  31;  *her-en,*  92;  *lov-en, folw-en,* 93; *wil-en,* 139; *forwerp-en,* 149, 155.  In Chaucer, this *-en* often becomes *-e.*   This suffix is, of course, most common in the *third* person; but it may occur in the first or second person; exx. *wit hav-en,* we-two have, 7; *wit shull-en,* 73.

**13.  Final *-es* in the Ormulum.**   Final *-es* always forms a distinct syllable.   It has three distinct values.

(*a*) It marks *the genitive case singular* of substantives. Exx. *flesh-es,* 2; *Godd-es,* 5; *gospell-es,* 54, 58, 60, 114, 118, 124; *folk-es,* 116; *Crist-es,* 152.

(*b*) It marks *the plural of substantives.*   Exx. *word-es,* 42, 52, 54, 58, 63, 102.

(*c*) It is *an adverbial ending* (originally a gen. sing.). Exx. *twy-es,* 104; *ell-es,* 108.  The *s*-sound is still preserved in our modern *twi-ce, el-se.*

**14.  Final *-e* in the Ormulum.**   I only include here such as happen to occur in our extract.   In substantives, it marks (*a*) the *nom.* or *acc.* of certain nouns, as will be more clearly shown hereafter; (*b*) the *dative* case; (*c*) the *genitive* case, in rare instances.

(*a*) The following may be considered as examples of the *nominative* or *accusative; trouth-e,* 4; *will-e,* 12; *lor-e,* 14, 70; *help-e,* 26, 90; *modiness-e,* 78, 156; *sinn-e,* 84; *or-e,* 152.

(*b*) The following are *datives; kynd-e,* 2; *wys-e,* 6; *fram-e,* 18; *mess-e,* 32; *ned-e,* 36; *end-e,* 90, 127, 144; *might-e,* 119; *spech-e,* 130; *er-e,* 133; *hert-e,* 134; *tung-e,* 135; *ded-e,* 136.

(*c*) The following is an example of the *genitive* case ; *sowl-e*, 138. The explanation of this form depends upon the fact that the A.S. *sāwel* is a *feminine* sb., of which the genitive case is *sāwl-e*, with a final *-e*. In ll. 36, 148, *sowl-e* may represent the genitive *plural*; from A.S. *sāwla*.

The curious word *rym-e* in l. 44 should not be over-looked ; here the final *-e* depends upon etymology. The word is not English, but borrowed from the O.F. [Old French] *rimë*, a dissyllabic word ; the Ital. form is *rima*.

(*d*) Final *-e* marks the *definite adjective*, as distinct from the indefinite. An adjective is said to be definite, when preceded by the definite article or by a demonstrative or possessive pronoun. Exx. *the thridd-e*, 6 ; *that loth-e*, 75 ; *this first-e*, 100. Or it marks *the dative case*; as in *full-e*, 119.

(*e*) It is the sign of the *plural of an adjective.* Exx. *myn-e*, 52 ; *all-e*, 30, 91 ; *fel-e*, 102 ; *Cristen-e*, 122.

(*f*) Final *-e* is the mark of various parts of the verb ; thus it occurs in the present tense singular of the indicative and subjunctive moods. Exx. 1 p. s. indic. *hav-e*, 13, 25, 29, 112. 3 p. s. subj. *wryt-e*, 97, 104, 107 ; *lok-e*, 103 ; *wil-e*, 111.

(*g*) A most important use of the final *-e* is when it marks *the past tense of a weak verb*, i. e. of a verb of which the past participle ended in *-ed, -d*, or *-t*. Exx. *sett-e*, 10 ; *might-e*, 17 ; *wold-e*, 20, 131 ; *shold-e*, 24, 133, 135. We should notice that, on the contrary, there is (usually) *no* final *-e* at the end of the past participle[1]; as in *forth-ed*, 12 ; *wend*, 13 ; *len-ed*, 16 ; *broght*, 28 ; *samn-ed*, 29 ; *set*, 41 ; *ek-ed*, 46 ; &c. The contrast between *Saint Austin sett-e* (10) and *I hav-e set* (41) is very clearly marked. Cf. G. *ich dachte* with the pp. *gedachte*.

---

[1] Exceptions are when the pp. is used as an adjective, in conjunction with *plural* substantives ; or is used as an adjective in the definite form.

C

(*h*) Final *-e* frequently marks *an adverb*. Exx. *yern-e,*
20; *ther-onn-e*, 38; *oft-e*, 62, 68; *swyth-e*, 71.

(*i*) A final *-e* frequently represents an A.S. vowel-ending,
in various parts of speech. Thus the form *hir-e* (86) represents A.S. *hir-a*, of them, their; and *theyr-e* (142, 148)
represents A.S. *þær-a*, or (more strictly) the equivalent
Icel. *þeirr-a*, of them, their.

(*k*) Besides the above instances of the final *-e*, used as
a distinct syllable for some grammatical reason, we must
not omit to notice that a syllabic *-e-* may occur in the
middle of a word in such instances as *blith-e-ly*, 92, 131.
The same peculiarity is found in Chaucer's English.

**15.** The above examples are quite sufficient to establish
the principle, that it is impossible to scan the Ormulum
until one has learnt the grammar; and the same is true
with regard to Chaucer. We have also learnt, even from
the examination of only a short passage, what are the chief
cases in which a final *-en*, *-es*, or *-e* increases by one the
number of syllables in a word. To recapitulate, we observe
that a final *-en* marks, in the Ormulum, an infinitive, a
gerund, or a strong past participle; whilst, in Chaucer, the
same parts of the verb are marked, indifferently, by *-en* or
*-e*. Next, that a final *-es* marks the genitive case or the
plural of substantives, or constitutes an adverbial ending.
And lastly, that a final *-e* marks sometimes a nominative
or accusative, sometimes a dative, and occasionally a genitive case of a substantive; and sometimes, as in *rym-e*, its
value is etymological. In adjectives, it marks the definite
form or the plural. In verbs, it occurs in the present, in
the past tense plural, and in the (weak) past tense singular.
It is common in adverbs; and (it may be added) appears
in such a preposition as *without-e* (mod. E. *without*), which
is also spelt *without-en*; as well as in such words as *hir-e*,
their, *theyr-e*, their, answering to A.S. *hir-a*, Icel. *þeirr-a*.
We also meet with a syllabic *-e-* before the suffix *-ly*.

# CHAPTER II

## THE TEXT

**16.** BEFORE we can make a similar investigation with regard to the Canterbury Tales, we must first of all consider *what text* we may accept as being sufficiently correct. The two latest and most accessible texts are those edited by myself and by Mr. Pollard, known as The Student's Chaucer and as the Globe edition respectively. In a recent review of the latter it was asserted, with that perfect recklessness which is born of irresponsibility, that there is a wide difference between the two. The text in the Student's Chaucer was distinguished as being 'eclectic,' whilst that in the Globe edition was called 'scientific.' What these words were intended to imply, I have no idea; but it is obviously necessary to find out, if possible, in what this notable difference consists. As I propose to examine the metre of Part I of the Squieres Tale in particular, it is obviously necessary to collate the texts beforehand. This I have accordingly done, and present the reader with the results, denoting the Student's edition by S., and the Globe edition by G.

**17.** (*a*) S. usually makes a phonetic distinction between the short *i* in *him* and the long *i* in *lyth* (he lies), denoting the latter by *y*. This distinction is not observed in G., which has *hym* and *lyth*, both with *y*. It makes no difference in the reading or the scansion, but it affects the pronunciation.

(*b*) Several slight differences of spelling occur, such as
S. *can*, G. *kan*; S. *fresh*, G. *fressh*. We may especially
note S. *e*, *o*, G. *ee*, *oo*, as in the following cases, S. *feste*,
G. *feeste*; S. *hote*, G. *hoote*. In such cases, I see no gain
in the retention of such spellings as *kan*, *fressh*, *feeste*, *hoote*;
but these are only very small matters of opinion, which in
no way affect the reading or scansion, or even the pronunciation.

(*c*) G. has numerous examples of what may be called the
'idle' or archaic final *-e*. Examples occur in such monosyllabic words as *youre*; *sire*; *hire* (also frequently *hir*);
also in *lóngynge* (39); *présentes* for *présents* (174), dissyllabic
because the accent is thrown back; *ascéndynge* (264);
*hévene* (272). As there is a special mark employed in G.
for denoting when the final *-e* constitutes a syllable, and the
mark in all such cases is absent, the text in G. absolutely
coincides in reality (in this respect) with the text in S.
It seemed to me to be a far simpler plan to write *your*, *sir*,
*longing*, *hir*, &c., in accordance with the true pronunciation, rather than to retain such letters merely for the sake
of saying that they do not count. Thus, in l. 1, G. has
'Squier, come neer,' as in MS. E.; but, considering that
'come' here answers to A.S. *cum*, and was monosyllabic
from the very first in every Teutonic language (for it is the
imperative singular), it is far less confusing to the reader
to correct the scribe's false spelling, and to print 'com
neer,' as in S.

As this is the point wherein which G. and S. differ most,
we gather that by a 'scientific' text is meant one in which
the final *-e* is retained in places where the scribe inserted
it wrongly as well as in places where he inserted it
rightly[1].

[1] A particularly clear case is in l. 64, where G. has :—'Thanne
wolde it occupie a someres day'; where *Thanne* is an error for *Than*
(as in MSS. Cp. Pt. Ln. Hl.).

(*d*) There are a few real differences of reading; the chief are in l. 20 (where G. substitutes the reading of MS. Hn., as in my Six-text edition); l. 86, G. *spoken*, S. *spoke*; l. 96, G. *comen*, S. *come*; 165, G. *Strike*, S. *Stroke*; 173, G. *unto*, S. *to*; 184, G. *ne*, S. *or*; 201, G. *al the*, S. *the*; 226, G. *hyë*, S. *maister*; 260, G. *on alle*, S. *alle*; 266, G. *Cambyuskan*, S. *this Cambinskan*; 324, G. *stondë*, S. *abyde*. We need not discuss these points, as they will not affect our conclusions.

**18.** I have made the most of the above differences, because so ridiculous a conclusion has been drawn from them. There must always be a 'personal equation,' owing to differences of editorial methods. But there is *no* such difference as has been alleged. When the above small points are allowed for, the texts in S. and G. agree in the minutest particulars of spelling, being in fact both founded on the Ellesmere MS. There is nothing that points either to an 'eclectic' text on the one hand, or to a 'scientific' text on the other; and, if a critic finds amusement in the use of such unmeaning words, there is at any rate no reason at all why their application might not have been transposed. Had S. been called a 'scientific' text, and G. an 'eclectic' one, we should have been just as wise as ever.

The above collation has been made, of course, solely for the purposes of future argument; and, in order to eliminate all possible sources of error, I have taken the precaution to prepare my rules by help of text S., and to revise them by help of text G. The reader can then use which ever text happens to come most handy, and the results will be precisely the same. The fact that all such slight differences have been noted and allowed for will serve to show all the more clearly that the rules for scansion are perfectly sound, and cannot be set aside by groundless cavils.

**19.** In entering upon the question as to the scansion of

The Squieres Tale, it is plainly worth while to take as
a probable source of guidance such rules as have been
already shown to exist in the case of the Órmulum. It
would also be a good thing if we could ascertain beforehand whether it is probable that such rules hold for *all*
the Tales in the series, as well as for the Squieres Tale only.

It is reassuring to find that this wide and extensive
investigation has actually been made, once and for all. The
standard work upon the subject is the wonderfully diligent,
comprehensive and searching essay entitled ' Observations
on the Language of Chaucer,' by F. J. Child, Professor in
Harvard College. It is surprising to find that this sound
piece of work is dated as far back as June 3, 1862. A brief
account of what this essay accomplished will be found to
put the whole matter in a clearer light.

**20.** The essay was founded on Thomas Wright's text of
the Canterbury Tales, which was issued at first for the
Percy Society in 1847–51, and afterwards reissued in a
half-crown volume, without date. Professor Child's essay
was founded on the assumption that this was a trustworthy
text, which is far from being the case ; still, in covering the
whole ground, many errors were eliminated by comparison,
and by reference to the rules of Anglo-Saxon grammar, of
which Professor Child was a complete master. The following passage from his introductory remarks will be read with
interest, and is essential for our purpose.

**21.** ' The Harleian MS. No. 7334 was made the basis of
a new edition of the Canterbury Tales, prepared by
Mr. Wright for the Percy Society (1847–51). This manuscript was " collated throughout " with the Lansdowne MS.
851, in the British Museum (which seems to be [and is]
Tyrwhitt's W.), and as far as the Wife of Bath's Tale with
two others. The collations, however, do not extend to
grammatical minutiæ, and though the editor informs us
that he has corrected many obvious errors, *we may regard*

*the text as essentially a reprint of the Harleian MS.* 7334 [1].
As such it is of great value, but it is, nevertheless, by
no means a satisfactory, or even a comfortably readable
text. The number of manifest errors still left is considerable, the number of probable ones enormous. Hundreds
of lines are incomplete, and long passages exhibit much
irregularity of language and metre. On the other hand,
there are long passages which appear to be but very slightly
corrupted from the original, the metre being regular, and
certain plain grammatical laws uniformly observed.'

22. I shall now produce a passage from Mr. Wright's
preface, in which he makes certain reflexions on the edition
by Tyrwhitt in 1775–8 (reprinted in 1798, 1822, 1830,
1845). It is not a little instructive, if read in the light of
the footnotes which I here subjoin.

'Tyrwhitt's entire ignorance of the grammar of the
language of Chaucer is exhibited in almost every line [2],
few of which could possibly have been written by the poet
as he has printed them [3]. It need only be stated, as an instance of this, that in the preterites of what the modern
Teutonic philologists term the strong verbs . . . Tyrwhitt has
invariably placed a verb in the plural with a noun in the
singular [4]. Examples of this (in the verbs *to bear*, of which
the correct forms were, sing. *bar*, pl. *bare* [5]; *to come*, sing.

---

[1] The italics are mine. Prof. Child had no means of knowing, at
the time, that this assumption was hardly justified. For further
remarks, see § 23.

[2] Tyrwhitt wrote an Essay on the Language and Versification of
Chaucer, which show that he at any rate was alive to the value
of A. S. grammar. We cannot, however, accept such statements as
that 'the nouns adjective had lost all distinction of gender, case, or
number.'

[3] A gross exaggeration; very many lines are correct.

[4] Not invariably; Tyrwhitt has *slep*, Prol. 98; *carf*, Prol. 100.

[5] The more 'correct' form is *beren*; both *baren* and *beren* occur in
Chaucer, though not (perhaps) in the C. T. Wright was thinking of
Prol. 105, 108, where Tyrwhitt has *he bare*.

*cam*, pl. *come*; *to swear*, sing. *swor*, pl. *swore*; *to give*, sing. *gaf*, pl. *gave*[1]; *to speak*, sing. *spak*, pl. *spake*; *to rise*, sing. *ros, roos*, pl. *rose*[2] . . .) occur in almost every sentence[3]. In the verb *to sit*, of which the pt. s. and pl. was *sette*[4], Tyrwhitt has substituted *set*, a form which did not exist; and in the same manner, in the verb *to creep*, he has given pt. s. *crept*[5], when the forms were sing. *creep, crope*[6], pl. *crope*. In the same manner, Tyrwhitt has in most instances substituted the plural of adjectives for the singular, and the inflected cases of nouns for the nominative[7], besides an infinity of errors in the orthographical forms of the language[8].'

**23.** We thus see that Wright's account of Tyrwhitt's text is not very accurate, and that he was himself wholly ignorant of many facts which it much concerned him to know. But the worst point about his text is that it frequently does *not* represent the Harl. MS. with fidelity. He himself tells us that he has corrected it where the scribal error is obvious, as when, for instance, the word *moralitee* has been turned into *more ryalte*, and that in such a case he has made the alteration without giving any

---

[1] We should expect sing. *yaf*, pl. *yeve*; he refers to Prol. 177, where Tyrwhitt has *He yafe*, Wright *He gaf*, and the Harl. MS. *ȝaf* ( = *yaf* ).

[2] This is truly astonishing; the pl. form is *rise(n)*, but it does not occur. So also the pl. of *rood* (he rode) is *riden*, as printed by Tyrwhitt (and by Wright!) in Prol. 825 (or 827).

[3] Yet strong verbs in the pt. t. are rare.

[4] Not so; the pt. t. was *sat*, pl. *sēte*. And both Tyrwhitt and Wright (!) have *sat*, Prol. 469 (or 471).

[5] But *crepen* had a double form for the pt. t. And Wright himself prints *crepte* in A. 4193 (or 4191).

[6] How so? The final *e* is not wanted, and I doubt if *croop* occurs.

[7] Yet, throughout Chaucer, strong fem. sbs. regularly present this very substitution. The gen. of A.S. *brȳd*, a bride, is *brȳde*; and Wright himself has *bryde* as a nom. case in l. 9764 (E 1890).

[8] It will be seen that the case is overdrawn, and that Wright knew but little better than his predecessor.

notice; but he unfortunately adds:—'in other instances, where a reading in the Harl. MS., although affording a tolerable meaning, has appeared to me a decided bad one, I have changed it for a better, always (when there is room for the least doubt) giving the original reading of the manuscript in a foot-note.' But this he *very rarely does*, so that the reader never knows what the MS. reading is. When the true state of the case became at last known, Dr. Furnivall printed the Harl. MS. with diplomatic exactitude, altering nothing, so that we now know exactly where we are [1]. It turns out that this celebrated but imperfect MS. is a most dangerous and uncertain guide. I quite agree with Mr. Pollard's account of it, which runs thus:— 'there can be no doubt that its readings are often extraordinarily careless, and even absurd. On the other hand, it has a number of readings . . . as good [as] or better than those found in any other MS., and many of them of a kind which it is very improbable that a copyist would have introduced in transcription. The most probable explanation seems to be that many of these readings represent Chaucer's own "second thoughts," introduced into a MS. which passed through his hand after the Tales were already in circulation, and that the Harleian MS. is a careless copy of this MS.' In a word, its chief merit lies in its containing some emendations from an 'inspired' source. Of this there is an excellent example in l. 8 of the Prologue, where the six MSS. of the 'Six-text Edition' all read *his half cours*, in defiance of grammar and scansion; whereas the Harl. MS. has *his halfe cours*, correctly.

**24.** It must be added, for the reader's information, that Mr. Wright's edition was long accepted as being almost the best possible, notwithstanding the verdict of Professor

---

[1] We learn, for example, that the MS. has lost eight leaves (which Wright calls 'a leaf or two'), containing F 617–1223 (608) lines, which are supplied by him *from Tyrwhitt's text*.

Child. Hence it came to be reproduced in the edition known as Bell's Chaucer; and the Preface to that edition contains the most astonishing statement that I ever remember to have met with during an experience of forty years. I refer to the following passage. 'It is proper to observe that, although the Harl. MS. has been adopted as the basis of this text, it has not been implicitly followed in all cases. As Mr. Wright found it necessary to depart occasionally from his original, so, in some instances, the reading of Mr. Tyrwhitt, when it bore internal evidence of authenticity, has been preferred in this edition. A few cases also occur in which the reading of the MS. has been restored, when it was thought that Mr. Wright had rejected it without sufficient reason ; but *all deviations* [the italics are mine] *either from Mr. Wright's edition, or from the original MS.*, are pointed out in the footnotes for the ultimate satisfaction of the reader.' It is a sufficient comment upon this statement to say that nearly all the footnotes are explanatory of words and phrases in the text, and that any note referring to a reading is of most rare occurrence. Thus, in vol. i. p. 141 (A 1637–1666), the sole note on the text merely states that '*they* is written for though,' in l. 1666, which is quite true. But the omissions are extraordinary ; for Mr. Wright's text here departs from the MS. no less than *seven times*, and the record of one of these deviations, pointed out in a footnote by Mr. Wright himself, is *not* reproduced. I give the other six cases (two are in one line) to show the singular vagaries of which the scribe of the Harl. MS. was capable, and how the editors dealt with them.

'And hereth him *comyng* in the greues '; A 1641.

*Comyng* is altered by Wright to *come russhyng*, as in the Ellesmere MS. See S. and G.

They foyneden ech at other longe ; 1654.

For *longe*, Wright has *wonder longe* (correctly). But *foyneden* is an error for *foynen*.

'In his fightyng were a wood lyoun'; 1656.

This is a most important case. Here the MS. is perfectly correct; for the first accent falls upon the word *In*, and the second on *fight-*, so that the line is perfect as it stands, affording one of the many instances in which a single accented syllable stands alone in the first foot. But Wright and Bell both insert *as* before *a wood*, obviously in order to make up the tale of ten syllables. This precious *as* was obtained from Tyrwhitt's edition; it does not occur in the original black-letter editions (1532–61), nor in any of (at any rate) the best MSS. That is to say, the text has been deliberately altered by both editors *without any notice whatever*[1]. This is altogether too bad.

'And as wilde boores gonne they smyte'; 1658.

Here Wright omits *And*, and inserts *togeder* (as in Tyrwhitt) before *smyte*. No notice is given, and the resulting line is simply hideous, viz. :—

'As wildè boorès gonnè they togeder smyte.'

The right reading is simple enough; for *togeder* read *to*.

'That frothen white as fome frothe wood'; 1659.

For *frothe* Wright has *for ire*, correctly. But why were we not told what the Harl. MS. really had? It is clear that the editor of Bell's edition simply took Wright's text for granted, without ever consulting the MS. in this passage. After telling us that 'all deviations from the original MS. are pointed out in the footnotes for the ultimate satisfaction of the reader,' he misses the above six variations in the course of only nineteen lines! Only five lines

---

[1] Yet Tyrwhitt expressly says, in a note on the passage :—'*As* has been inserted for the sake of the metre, but I am not satisfied with it'; which is a perfectly honest avowal.

further on Wright correctly altered *excused* (as in the MS.)
to *executeth*, adding the note—'the MS. Harl. reads *excused.*' But this note is actually suppressed! In both
editions, the reader is often deliberately befooled.

**25.** Truly the fates were strongly against the early
production of a good text of the Tales. All the black-letter
editions were very unsatisfactory, owing to their unphonetic
spelling. Urry's edition was much worse, and is quite
the worst on record. Tyrwhitt trusted too much to the
old editions, and too little to the MSS. Wright took as
the basis of his text the faulty and treacherous Harleian
MS.; and Bell followed Wright blindly, exclaiming all the
while that he did so with open eyes. Thus it was that
Dr. Morris's edition (1866), though better than its pre-
decessors, was foredoomed to failure from two causes.
First of all, he trusted to the same MS., the badness of
which was as yet quite unsuspected; and secondly, the
plan of his book allowed him *no footnotes*, and this was
fatal. All he could do was to indicate, by printing words
*in italics*, the instances in which he had deviated from the
MS. But this was a very poor expedient, and in many
cases, even the use of these italics was *not observed*. It
is necessary that the reader should know this; for the
failure of these italics is most misleading. It is sufficient
to refer to the instances above discussed. In l. 1641,
Morris retains *comyng*, so that there are (rightly) no italics
in this instance. In l. 1654, he prints 'wonder' in roman
type, as if it were in the MS., which it is not. In l. 1656,
he has 'as' in roman, as if it were in the MS.; but, as
explained above, it is neither there nor elsewhere, which
is most distracting. In l. 1658, he has *to* in italics, because
it is substituted for *togeder*; but he also (quite correctly)
omits *And* at the beginning of the line, although it was
quite impossible to say so; for there was no way open to
him for indicating omissions. In l. 1659, he rightly has

*for ire* jn italics.　Out of five alterations in the course of only six lines, *two* are indicated and *three* are not.

**26.** The reader has now all the facts before him. Professor Child's wonderful essay was founded, as he was well aware, on faulty materials, as far as the text was concerned.　But he had, on the other hand, large means of controlling it, owing to his intimate acquaintance with etymological and grammatical details.　Moreover, the Tales form a poem of great length ; Tyrwhitt's edition has 17,385 lines.　Hence it came to pass that at least 10,000, and probably more than 15,000 lines were quite correct, and could be scanned perfectly; and this was, practically, sufficient.　Professor Child obtained all the more important results, and not many have since been added.　As we have now, however, a text of far higher accuracy, easily accessible either in S. (the Student's edition) or G. (the Globe edition), the differences between which (as shown above) are really very slight[1], it is worth while to give all the grammatical rules *in extenso*, from an analysis of Part I. of the Squieres Tale, with a reference in each case to the numbered sections of Child's essay.

I also give the references to the sections of the accurate and important work by B. ten Brink, entitled Chaucers Sprache und Verskunst, Leipzig, 1884.　The results are much the same.

---

[1] Only the reader must remember that a final *-e*, in G., *except when it ends a line*, is to be treated as idle or non-existent, unless specially marked as being pronounced.　The final *-e*, in S., usually takes care of itself, and should be sounded.

# CHAPTER III

## ANALYSIS OF THE SQUIERES TALE

**27.** THE scansion of Chaucer's lines depends upon their pronunciation; and the pronunciation is largely affected by the use of grammatical inflexions, many of which are now obsolete.

It will be understood that Chaucer can only be read *correctly* by those who are thoroughly acquainted with Middle-English sounds, especially those of the vowels. A brief account of these sounds is given in my six-volume edition, vol. vi, beginning at p. xxv; in my Introduction to Chaucer's Man of Lawes Tale; and at pp. 12–14 of the Introduction to my shilling edition of Chaucer's Prologue. It is not necessary to repeat the information here, because the Canterbury Tales can be scanned even if a modern pronunciation be adopted, if only the grammatical inflexions be duly regarded. But a full account of these is obviously necessary. The various uses of M.E. [Middle English] inflexion are numbered below, for our convenience in future reference.

**28. Final -es.** Final *-es* usually forms a distinct syllable. (Exceptions will be noted afterwards.) As in the Ormulum (see § 13) it has three distinct values.

1. It marks *the genitive case singular of substantives*: Child, § 21; ten Brink, §§ 200, 204, 212. In the following examples, the numbers refer to the lines of the Squieres Tale, the first Tale in Group F. The references are

available for either S. (Student's Chaucer) or G. (Globe edition).

Martes, 50, som*e*res, 64, Grekes, 209, Canaceës, 247, kinges, 299.

In the word 'som*e*res,' the former *e* is here printed in italics to show that it is slurred over, and does not count in the verse; the word is pronounced nearly as 'som'res'; in romic notation (sum·rez).

2. It marks the *plural of substantives* : Child, § 22 ; ten Brink, §§ 202, 206, 210. (In the following examples, the suffix is printed in italics when the pronunciation of it is light, and hardly counts in the verse; and such cases will be explained.)

Armes, 23, swannes, 68, mínstrallés, 78, thinges, 78, lordes, 91, wordes, 103, woundes, 155, winges, 208, gestes, 211, armes, 213, festes, 219, doutes, 220, thinges, 222, 227, angles, 230, bokes, 235, medicynes, 244, ringes, 249, spyces, 291, 294, lordes, 304, 345.

Sewes, 67, heronsewes, 68, houres, 117, shoures, 118, fantasyës, 205, poetryës, 206, lyves, 233, prospectýves, 234, daunces, 283, countenaunces, 284, dissimulinges, 285, aperceyvinges, 286. All in the latter set come at the end of a line, and are therefore left unmarked in G. ; but these examples are just as real as the rest, and add the great beauty of a feminine or double rime, such as Chaucer and Dante much affected.

Son*es*, 29, foul*es* (G. fow*eles* = fow'l*es*), 53, hed*es* (G. hedd*es*), 203, witt*es*, 203, skil*es*, 205.

These examples should be particularly noticed; they are all dissyllabic like the rest. In full, the lines run thus :—

'Haddë two son*ës* | on Elpheta his wyf'; 29.

'For which the foul*ës* | agayn the sonnë shenë'; 53.

'As many hed*ës* | as many witt*ës* ther been'; 203.

'And maden skil*ës* | after hir fantasýës'; 205.

Note that *sones*, *foules*, *hedes*, *skiles*, all occur at the caesural pause, where an extra syllable in the verse is fully permissible, according to a licence which adds variety to the measure. This was common in Old French Verse (see Toynbee's Specimens of Old French, Introd. § 26), and is of frequent occurrence in all English verse. Compare, for example, the following lines :—

'At least two glass*es*. | The time 'twixt six and now';
Tempest, i. 2. 240.

'In their distrac*tions*. | They now are in my power';
Temp. iii. 3. 90.

'Obey, and be attent*ive*. | Canst thou remember';
Temp. i. 2. 38.

'And promised for *him*. | And Arthur made him knight';
Pelleas and Ettarre.

Of course it is desirable that the extra syllable thus introduced should not be too full or heavy. Chaucer has been so careful of this that in all the four instances cited above the final *-es* is followed by a *vowel*. In l. 203, we not only have *hedës* at the caesura, but also *wittës ther been* at the end of the line. This creates no special difficulty; it is paralleled by a line in The Tempest (i. 2. 122):—

'To me invet*erate*, heark*ens* my brother's suit.'

It is only necessary to observe here, that the student must allow for elisions and for extra syllables at the caesura (and even elsewhere) if he means to master Chaucer's versification[1]. Patience and docility are required as well as a good ear; and above all, a mind not obstinately adherent to unfounded prepossessions. Nineteenth-century ideas are sometimes wofully misleading. I can give no

---

[1] There are pedants who will never understand this. When they come to l. 148 of the Prologue—But sor-e weep she | if oon of hem were deed—they ignore the caesura, cut down the eleven syllables to ten, and insist on saying *shif*!

better advice to the learner than that he should read the
lines *much* more slowly and deliberately than he is wont
to read modern poems. Gabble and hurry are ruin to
Middle-English verses.

This is perhaps a good place for noting that words *of
French origin* form the plural in -*s*, rather than in -*es*, when
the suffix follows an unstressed syllable, and often when
it follows a syllable in which the stress is only secondary;
and this suffix does *not* add a syllable to the word: Child,
§ 22. Exx. présents (G. presentes, where the third *e* is
idle), 174; jógelours, 219, refléxioùns, 230, mírours, 234,
&c. In the same way, the plural of *lady*, though written
*ladyes*, remains dissyllabic, simply because the singular
*lády* is dissyllabic already and has the stress on the former
syllable; for if the word were made trisyllabic, an awkward
secondary accent would be thrown on the suffix. Hence
*lórdës* and *ládyes* (laa·diiz) are both dissyllabic, as in l. 304.
Cf. Child, § 22; ten Brink, § 226.

3. Final -*es* occurs *as an adverbial suffix*: Child, § 73;
cf. ten Brink, § 249.

Certes, 2, 196, elles, 118, algates, 246, thennes, 326, 327.
And observe elle*s* (before a vowel), 209.

**29. Final -en.** We saw (§ 12) that final -*en* in the
Ormulum marks (*a*) the infinitive: (*b*) the gerund: (*c*) the
strong pp.: (*d*) the pres. pl. or pt. pl. And we find
examples of all these in Chaucer.

4. Final -*en* marks *the infinitive mood*: Child, § 60;
ten Brink, § 190.

Discryven, 40, tellen, 63, 67, reporten, 72, percen, 237,
devysen, 282, rehercen, 298. But *fleen* (122) is a monosyllable (A.S. *fléon*).

5. Final -*en* marks *the gerund*: Child, § 60; ten Brink,
§ 190.

To voyden, 188, to gauren, 190, to maken, 254, to
ryden, 315, to clepen, 331.

6. Final *-en* marks the *pp. of a strong verb* : Child, § 61 ; ten Brink, § 196.

Geten, 56, knowen, 280, y-knowen, 256.

7. Final *-en* marks the *plural of the present or past tense* : Child, §§ 52, 55 ; ten Brink, §§ 192, 194.

*Present pl.* tellen, 69, wayten, 88, shapen, 214, pleyen, 219, knowen, 235, spek*en*, 243, drawen, 252, wondren, 258, demen, 261, sownen, 270, dauncen, 272, soupen, 297. *Second person*, ye moten, 316 ; *subj.* ye slepen, 126.

*Past plural, strong*: seten, 92, writen, 233; *weak* : murmur*en*, 204 ; maden, 205, seyden, 248, wondred*en*, 307.

8. Final *-en* occurs in *prepositions and adverbs* : Child, § 72.

Withouten, 101, 121, 125, 180.

**30. Final (syllabic) -e.** We saw, in § 14, that the final *-e*, in the Ormulum, marks many grammatical inflexions, occurring in (*a*) the nom. or acc. of a sb. ; (*b*) the dative ; (*c*) the genitive ; (*d*) the def. adj. ; (*e*) the pl. adj. ; (*f*) the verb, 1 pr. s. ; (*g*) the pt. s. of a weak verb ; (*h*) an adverb ; (*i*) some A.S. suffix of varying character. There is also (*k*) a medial *-e-*, constituting a syllable. The grammatical functions of final *-e* in Chaucer are of a similar character. The parts of speech will be considered separately.

**31. Substantives.** The forms of sbs. in A.S. are not a sure guide to the pronunciation of Chaucer, unless it be first of all understood that the practice of his day differed from that in use before the Conquest to a limited extent, owing to a certain confusion of the various cases of the substantive that had naturally come about in course of time. The chief points of difference are really very easy to understand, and are fully discussed in the General Introduction to my six-volume edition of Chaucer, §§ 68–76, to which I must beg leave to refer the reader for further information. The object of this treatise is merely to give such elementary information as may suffice for determining the Chaucer Canon.

The principal contradiction, in the practice of Chaucer's time, to A.S. usage occurs in strong monosyllabic substantives of the feminine gender. In A.S. the sb. *lār*, lore, was thus declined in the singular. Nom. *lār*; gen. dat. acc. *lār-e*. If this practice had been implicitly followed, we should have had, in M.E., the following: Nom. *loor*; gen. dat. acc. *lor-e*. Of course the inevitable happened ; the two forms *loor* and *lor-e* were at one time both in use, but the tendency was towards confusion and simplification. The monosyllabic *loor* only occurred in the nominative, and was therefore less frequent. Consequently it perished, and only *lor-e* survived. Hence it is that *lor-e* is the sole type for all cases in Chaucer. At a still later date, the form *lor-e* lost its final *-e*, and became monosyllabic, as at the present day. This is well worth remembering, because it is a common belief that our mod. E. *lore* is ' derivèd from the A.S. *lār*.' This may be good enough for practical purposes, but is obviously false. The nom. case *lār* is the sole case of the A.S. sb. which the modern form does NOT represent !

When this clear and inevitable exception has been allowed for, it may be stated, generally, that, in all words of *native* origin, the declensional forms in A.S. are a fairly safe guide to those in Chaucer. As a rule, most substantives are dissyllabic, in all their cases ; the chief and obvious exception being the strong masculines and neuters which formed their nominatives and accusatives alike, and thereby held their ground. Exx. *ooth*, oath, *ring*, *arm* (of the body), *erl*, earl, *mouth*, *dreem*, dream, *boon*, bone, *fyr*, fire, *wyf*, wife, *day*, *path*, *staf*, *ship*, *writ*, net, *bed*, *wed*, pledge, *worm*, *deel*, part, *dint*, *loon*, loan ; &c.

We may particularly notice the dative case singular. In A.S., we have datives in *-e* (sometimes *-we*), *-a*, *-u*, *-an* ;

D 2

all of these produced M.E. -*e* ; and hence we gain the three following (empirical) rules.

(*a*) Neglecting stems in -*r*, and such words as show mutation, every dative case ends in -*e* in early M.E.

(*b*) Every accusative resembles either the nominative or the dative in early M.E. ; if the former, it either may or may not take final -*e* ; if the latter, it has it naturally.

(*c*) In Chaucer's time, these substantival inflexions were rapidly going out of use, so that he frequently *drops* the -*e* of the dative case.

The general rule for the preservation of the dative -*e* is that it was preserved in particular phrases which were in common use, such as *a-bed-de*, for A.S. *on bedde*, in bed ; and such phrases have been called 'petrified phrases.' Of course this is a very fair guide, but the statement that Chaucer sometimes retains the dative -*e* is just as true, and in some instances preferable. When Chaucer speaks of a dove as sitting *on a bern-e* (C 397), it is somewhat grandiloquent to call 'on a barn' a petrified phrase. To a plain man, it looks more like a dative after *on*. However, the net result is the same.

I now proceed to enumerate the instances of final -*e* in the Squieres Tale, as occurring in substantives.

9. *Substantives of A.S. origin ; nom. and acc.* : Child, §§ 1–18 ; ten Brink, §§ 199–211.

Wille, 1 (A.S. *willa*), sted', 115, 193, stede, 124, stede, 170 (A.S. *stēda*), tale, 6, 102 (A.S. *talu*), herte, 120, herte, 138 (A.S. *heorte*, acc. *heortan*), bote, 154 (A.S. *bōt*, f., gen. dat. acc. *bōte*), sonne, 170 (A.S. *sunna*) ; also sone, 31 (A.S. *sunu*), mete, 70 (A.S. *mete*).

10. *Substantives of F. origin ; nom., acc., and dat.* : Child, § 19 ; ten Brink, § 222. Sbs. of F. origin usually keep the O.F. form, so that feminine sbs. often have final -*e*. But it is to be noted, that the final -*e* in F. words is of a weak character, and is frequently dropped, though the

poet often contrives that the word shall come at the cæsura. Centre, 22, diademe, 43, diademe, 60, corage, 22, person', 25, signe, 51, servyse, 66, nobleye, 77, mérveill', 87, ordre, 92, reverenc', 93, obeisaunce, 93, contenaunce, 94, curteisye, 95, fairye, 96, messáge, 99, form', 100, langáge, 100, vic', 101, &c. Striking instances are: cause, 185, Troye, 210, Rome, 231. Notice, on the other hand, how the -e is often suppressed if the accent is thrown back; thus sérvice is only dissyllabic, 297. (But note sérvic-è, Prologue, 122.)

Chaucer often employs French words at the end of the line, for the sake of the feminine rime. Thus *diademe* rimes with *deme*, of native origin, 43; *nobleye* with *pleye*, 77; *entente* with *mente*, 107; &c.

11. *Substantives of A.S. origin; datives*: Child, §§ 13, 14; ten Brink, §§ 201, 205, 209.

Datives are frequently found after the prepositions *at, by, for, in, of, on, to, unto, upon.*

Ex. in the halle, 92, in the wounde, 165. The following may be considered as occurring in common phrases: in speche, 94, in mynde, 109, at your heste, 114, in drede, 212. And in the following, even the nom. case is dissyllabic, so that the dat. presents nothing distinctive: tyme, 74, tonge, 35, sonne, 53, grene, 54, dore, 80, thomb', 83, thombe, 148, syde, 84, met', 173, ere, 196, ende, 224. Tyde, 142, is properly a dative form, after *ageyn*.

The form *rōt-e* in l. 153 is worth attention. It is a fem. sb. of Norse origin (cf. Icel. nom. dat. acc. *rōt*, gen. *rōt-ar*. But it was of course conformed to the E. declension of the fem. sb. *bōt*, and thus acquired a final -e in the dative case, as in the second line of the famous General Prologue and in the present instance.

12. *Substantives of A.S. origin; genitives*: Child, § 16; ten Brink, §§ 208, 212.

These genitives belong to strong feminine substantives, except in a few cases, where they belong to substantives

of the weak declension. But most of the latter had a new
M.E. genitive in *-es.* Ex. halle, 80 (A.S. *healle*, gen. of *heall*,
str. fem.).

**32. Adjectives.** The four next sub-sections relate to
adjectives.

13. The definite form is used when the adj. is preceded
by *the, this, that,* or a possessive pronoun : Child, § 32 ;
ten Brink, § 235.

The hote, 51, the yonge, 54, the thridde, 76, the heighe,
85, 98, 176, his olde, 95, this same, 124, his newe, 140,
hir moste, 199, the loude, 268, the grete, 306. So *thilke*
for *the ilke*, 162. So even with French adjectives, as : his
queynte, 239 ; this strange, 89 (*strange* being, however,
etymologically dissyllabic) ; your excellente, 145 (though
*excellente* may here be intended to mark the feminine
gender) ; the platte, 164.

Observe that this extension of the adjectival form, in
native words, is practically limited to such as are etymologically monosyllabic, as *hoot, yong, heigh, old,* &c. In
dissyllabic words, the final *-e* soon fell away. Hence
*th'éldeste*, 30, should rather have been written *th'eldest.*
Cf. *this lusty*, 142 ; so also *the gentil*, 265 (where *gentil*
is French).

14. *Adjectives of F. origin* : ten Brink, § 239. Some
of these end in final *-e* owing to their etymology. A few
monosyllabic adjectives take final *-e* when used definitely.
But the final *-e* was weaker than in native words, and is
sometimes lost.

This noble, 12, 28, riche, 19, 61, benigne, 52, sólempn',
61, pryme, 73, commún', 107, my lige, 111, this solémpne,
111. L. 111 is a striking example :—

' My lig-e lord, on this solémpn-e day.'

15. *Adjectives ; plural* : Child, § 39 ; ten Brink, § 232.
The pl. of monosyllabic adjectives takes *-e* ; but not (usually)
of others, unless the syllable preceding *-e* is accented.

Olde, 69, 88, 206, 211, yong', 88, alle, 91, dep', 155, wyde, 155, grete, 219, somm', 225, sly*e*, 230, all*e*, 248, fresshe, 284. So also whiche, 30, swiche, 227 ; and divérse, 202 (of F. origin).

16. *Adjectives ; other inflexions* : Child, § 29 ; ten Brink, §§ 230, 235. Some adjectives take final -*e* because they preserve the A.S. form ; as, grene, 54 (A.S. *grēne*). The A.S. *þic* is, in the definite form, *se þicca* ; by confusion, Ch. uses *thikke* even when indefinite, as, 'a thikke knarre,' Prol. 549 ; hence, thikk*e*, 159. Note also liche, 62 (properly an inflected form) ; blyth*e*, 338 (A.S. *blīðe*). The notion of expressing a dative case by the inflexional -*e* extended even to adjectives ; e. g. alle, 15. Another peculiarity is the occasional use of -*e* to express a vocative ; e. g. O strong*e* god, Knightes Tale, A 2373.

**33. Verbs.** The five next sub-sections relate to verbs.

17. *Infinitive mood.* The ending -*e* simply results from -*en*, by loss of *n* ; see § 29 (4).

Sey', 4, rebelle, 5, telle, 6, undertak*e*, 36, spek', 41, occupy', 64, pleye, 78, amende, 97, 197, sem*e*, 102, soun', 105, ber*e*, 124, turn', 127, hyde, 141, here, 146, know', 151, answer', 152, knowe (*at the cæsura*), 154, kerv', 158, byte, 158, close, 165, here, 188, rede, 211, comprehende, 223 ; &c.

18. *Gerundial infinitive* ; -*e* for -*en* ; see § 29 (5).

To telle, 34, to devyse, 65, to biholde, 87, to pace, 120, to sore, 123, to were, 127, to winne, 214, to here, 271, to hye, 291.

To seyne, 314, to done, 334 : these are instances in which the A.S. final -*e* is preserved ; cf. A.S. *tō secganne*, *tō dōnne*. They are therefore quite distinct from the preceding ; see Child, § 60 ; ten Brink, § 190.

Observe that this gerundial -*e* is seldom elided.

19. *Strong verbs ; past participle* ; -*e* for -*en* ; see § 29 (6).

Holde, 70, spok' (G. spok*en*), 86, com' (G. com*en*), 96, bore, 178, knowe, 215, yswore, 325, ydraw*e*, 326, ybore, 326.

20. *Weak verbs; past tense.* In the case of weak verbs, which include a large number of verbs of Anglo-French origin, much depends upon the form and even upon the length of the stem. The standard suffix for the pt. t. is -*de*, and for the pp. -*d*; but this necessarily becomes -*te* (pp. -*t*) after a voiceless consonant and in some other cases, especially after *gh*. A third variety of form is caused by the frequent occurrence of -*e*- before the final -*de* (pp. -*d*), due, usually, to the A.S. form in -*ode*; and in long words especially, the form -*ede* is frequently reduced to -*ed*, or (by contraction) to -'*de* or -'*d*. This short explanation applies, practically, to all weak verbs.

The application of the above statement to the three classes of A.S. weak verbs, and to verbs of F. origin, is given in the six-volume edition, pp. lxxvii–lxxx, and need not be repeated here. The details are somewhat complex, but are easily understood by reference to an Anglo-Saxon grammar. Examples follow.

(*a*) Pt. t. in -*de*: deyde, 11 ; hadde (not here an auxiliary verb), 29, hadd*e*, 32, coud', 39, shold', 40, wold', 64, sholde, 102, 282, wende, 198, answérd', 228, seyd', 228, wolde, 237, coude, 283, leyd', 313. Loss of -*e* is often seen in the case of such very common words as *coud'*, *wold'*, *seyd'*.

(*b*) Pt. t. in -*te*: dwelt', 10, kept', 18, 26, highte, 30, 33, moste, 38, wroughte, 128, lighte, 169, broughte, 210, might', 227.

(*c*) Pt. t. in -*ed*: wérreyed, 10, . lakked, 16, sem*e*d or sem'd, 56, semed, 201, demed, 202, rowned, 216. Cf. preyed' (G. preydë), 311.

Note also the plurals murmur*e*den (= murmur'den), 204, wondred, 225; maden, 205, seyden, 231, wondred*en* (perhaps read wondred'), 307 ; cf. 225.

21. *Other verbal inflexions*: Child, §§ 48, 52 ; ten Brink, §§ 184, 188.

We find -*e* as the mark of the present indicative, both

in the 1st p. s. and in the pl.   This -*e* is weak, and sometimes dropped; but in the pres. subjunctive it is stronger,
and occurs in the 3rd person also.

(*a*) 1 pr. s. indic. deme, 44, trowe, 213, seye or sey, 289,
let', 290; (*b*) pr. pl. indic. recch', 71, lere, 104, smyte, 157,
mote, 164, 318, jangl', 220, trete, 220, jangle, 261, devyse,
261, gete, 343; (*c*) 1 and 3 sing. subj. (both pres. and past)
spek', 7, leste, 125, liste, 327; *pl.* reste, 126; *pt. s.* were,
195.

**34.** *Adverbs and prepositions.*   Child, §§ 69, 72; ten
Brink, § 246.

22. A.S. adverbs have commonly, in the positive degree,
the termination -*e*, which is usually preserved in Chaucer.

Yliche, 20, loude, 55, evermore, 124, brighte, 170, still',
171, therfore, 177, lowe, 216, bothe, 240, sore, 258, hye,
267, sone, 276, 333, namore, 314, namor', 343.

The final -*e* is even added, by analogy, in a few cases
where the A.S. form is without it; as herë, 144 (A.S.
*hër*)-

Sometimes a preposition ends in -*e*: bitwixe, 333.

23. We should also observe the instances in which -*e*-
forms a syllable, in adverbs ending in·-*ely*.

Richely, 90, solémpnely, 179, divérsely, 202.

**35.** It thus appears that there are some twenty-two grammatical uses of the suffixes -*es*, -*en*, -*e* in Chaucer; in all of
which the effect of the suffix is to add a syllable to the
word, thus affecting the scansion.   They are nearly all due
to the usages of A.S. grammar, or can be explained from
the original form of the A.S. word; hence they are easily
explicable by any one who is acquainted with the elementary
rules of A.S. and early M.E. grammar.

It has been already noted, however, that Chaucer
occasionally drops the final -*e* in cases where we might
expect it to be retained.   This has been denoted above
by printing the final -*e* as an italic letter.   Thus, l. 343

ends with—'ye get*e* namor' of me.' Here we have no means of deciding whether the -*e* in 'get*e*' was very slightly touched or whether it was suppressed altogether. The latter alternative is by no means unlikely, as Chaucer's use of the -*e* was certainly archaic, and the loss of it would not occasion any surprise. Nevertheless, the student is humbly advised to preserve this -*e* where he conveniently can[1]; even if it causes the introduction of three syllables in the place of two, it is not always a defect.

At the same time, it is quite certain that, in some *very common* words, the -*e* was often suppressed in spite of grammar. In fact, the retention of it would have seemed pedantic. It is highly advisable to notice a few words of this description.

For this particular purpose, it is best to consult the text in the Globe edition, as this contains a considerable number of examples of -*e* besides such as are required by the scansion. These, for the most part, fall into two distinct sets: (*a*) where the -*e* has *no* grammatical significance; (*b*) where its grammatical significance is of an archaic character.

Those in the former set need not detain us, as they can have nothing to do with the scansion, and are mere examples of bad spelling. A good instance is *come* in l. 1. It represents A.S. *cum*, and is a mere error for *com*; indeed, it is so written in the Hengwrt and Harleian MSS. Perhaps this is the only obvious clerical blunder on the part of the scribe of the Ellesmere MS. in the course of the 346 lines.

**36.** In considering those in the latter set, we are at once confronted by the fact that they are to some extent variable. But the variation is easy to understand. Take the case

---

[1] It is inconvenient to sound the *e* in *have* in l. 58. In such a case, it is easier to let it alone. So also *herde* = *herd*, 249.

of the words *hire* (her), *youre* (your). Their form depends
wholly upon stress. As a rule, these words were unstressed,
weak, enclitic. It then became impossible for them to
retain their dissyllabic form, and they easily passed into
*hir* and *your*.

Examples of their emphatic use are, of course, very
scarce. The emphatic forms seem to occur only at the
end of a line; in which case *hire* takes the form of *here*,
and forms a feminine rime, as in Cant. Tales, A 1421, 2057,
B 460, E 887, F 790. In all other cases, it is unemphatic,
and is reduced to *hir* (monosyllabic), as printed in S. In
G. it appears as *hir* or *hire* indifferently, which is needlessly
confusing, especially when it is noticed that the scribe of
Ellesmere MS. (in Sq. Tale, ll. 40, 55, 66, 68, 138, 147,
298) really writes 'hir,' with a useless flourish after the *r*
which has been wrongly expanded into 'hir*e*'; whilst in
other places the word is rightly printed 'hir.'

So also as to *youre*. This is only dissyllabic when
emphatic, and usually at the end of a line (as in the
Legend, 683); examples being scarce. It is commonly
monosyllabic, and is best printed as *your*; see ll. 1, 6, 113,
114, 120, 135, 136, 145, 167, 242.

The same is true of *sir* or *sire*; when emphatic, it is
*sir-ë*, as in Prol. 355. Elsewhere it is a mere monosyllabic
title, *sir*; see ll. 4, 314.

Similarly, *thanne* is usually reduced to *than*, 64; cf.
*whan*, 295.

Similarly, the word *wole*, when a mere auxiliary, becomes
*wol*, 75; cf. 323.

The word *were* (might be) is emphatic and dissyllabic
in l. 195, at the end of the line. The scribes mostly write
it *were* in all positions, as it is written now. But (as now)
it is commonly a mere monosyllable; see l. 182.

*Thise* occurs as the plural of *this*, and is written with
final -*e* to mark that it is plural. But it is monosyllabic

(probably pron. like mod. E. *these*); see ll. 206, 211, where, however, it occurs before vowels.

The word *coude* is very troublesome, as it varies without much reason; it is monosyllabic in ll. 128, 240 (and often elsewhere), but dissyllabic in l. 200, where it seems to have the especial meaning of 'was able to,' and may be considered emphatic. Cf. l. 283.

Other examples come under the rule that the final *-e* is frequently not sounded *when the preceding syllable is unstressed*.

Thus *manërë* is trisyllabic in l. 342, the stress being on the *second* syllable; but *mánere*, with the stress on the *first* syllable, is dissyllabic, and is better written *maner*, as in l. 329. Other examples are : *mánye*, the same as *mány*, 203; *félaw(e)*, 216; *ascéndynge*, 264; *hévene*, 271; *jálouse*, 286; cf. *júeles* (or *jéwels*), 341.

Similarly *présentes* is better spelt *presents*, 174; cf. *parementz*, 269.

In the same way, the medial *-e-* in *fowel*, 149, *foweles*, 53, means nothing; better spellings are *foul*, *foules*, or *fowl*, *fowles*.

I here recapitulate the results of this section. The words *hir(e)*, *your(e)*, *sir(e)*, *than(ne)*, *wol(e)*, *thise*, are here all monosyllabic; *coude* is of variable length; *máner(e)*, *mány(e)*, *félaw(e)*, *jálous(e)*, *júeles*, *présent(e)s*, *fów(e)les*, are all dissyllabic only; and *ascéndyng(e)* is trisyllabic only. As for *fow(e)l*, it is a mere monosyllable.

# CHAPTER IV

## VARIOUS RIME-TESTS

**37.** WE have seen that Chaucer has certain peculiarities of grammar, upon which the scansion of his lines largely depends. A sufficient sketch of these has been given.

But this is not all. He has also some peculiarities of pronunciation, which affect his rimes. The principal of these are his treatment of final *-y* or *-yë*, and of *-ight* or *-ight-e*; also his treatment of the close and open *o*, and of the close and open *e*. These will now be discussed separately.

**38. Rimes in -y and -yë.** By an exhaustive examination of all the rimes in the Canterbury Tales (and all other genuine works of Chaucer), Mr. Bradshaw established the following rules :—

1. Words that should, etymologically, end in *-y* (and not in *-y-e*) are found riming together, but never rime with a word of the other class.

2. Words that should, etymologically, end in *-y-e* (and not in *-y*) are found riming together, but never rime with a word of the other class.

An example of the former class is *sodeynly*, which rimes with all adverbs in *-ly*, and with words in *-y* generally; it has no final *-e*. On the other hand, M.E. *folye* (folly) is really *fol-y-e*, as it answers to the O.F. trisyllabic *folië* or *folyë*, Ital. *follia*, Span. and Port. *folia*.

Only *one* exception is known, and it admits of an easy

explanation.  In Sir Thopas (B 2089) *sir Gy* rimes with *chivalry'*, though the latter should be *chivalry-ë*.  But this is in a loose ballad-metre, not to be taken so seriously as usual.  Under the circumstances, *chivalrye* has been cut down to *chivalry'*, by a fair 'poetical licence.'

As the two above rules apply to the whole of the Tales, they are of course exemplified in Part I of the Squiers Tale.  Examples are :—

(1) *deliciously, sodeynly,* 79 ; *sodeinly, richely,* 89 ; *comunly, subtilly,* 221.

(2) *Tartary-e, Russy-e,* 1 ; *curteisy-e, fairy-e,* 95 ; *Lombardy-e, y-e* (eye), 193 ; *hy-e, minstralcy-e,* 267 ; *hy-e, y-e,* 273 ; *hy-e* (infin.), *melody-e,* 291.  Cf. Ital. *cortesia, Lombardia, melodia.*  So also the pl. forms *fantesy-es, poetry-es,* 205.

**39. Rimes in -ight, -yt.**  I have observed that, though the sound of *gh* was very faint in Chaucer (for it was fast disappearing), he nevertheless always regards it.  He never rimes a word that etymologically ends in *-ight* or *-ighte* with one in *-yt,* or *-yte.*  This is worth notice, for Lydgate does so freely ; in the very first stanza of The Complaint of the Black Knight we find *whyte* (white) riming with *brighte* (bright).

As this rule is general, it is exemplified in Part I of the Squiers Tale.  Examples are : (*a*) *bright, wight,* 137 ; *lighte, brighte,* 169 ; *knight, might,* 309 ; *wight, night,* 329 ; *knight, aright,* 335 ; (*b*) *smyte, byte,* 157.

Take notice that the mod. E. *delight* is misspelt, for it is of French origin ; Chaucer's form is *delyt,* riming with *appetyt,* E 1249.  Moreover, mod. E. has *two* words both spelt *plight,* one of which is misspelt.  When *plight* means 'to pledge,' it is of E. origin, and is spelt correctly ; but when it means 'condition,' it is of F. origin, and has no *gh.*  Thus Chaucer rimes the sb. *plyt* with *appetyt,* E 2335 ; and *plyte,* dat., with *wyte* (blame), G 952.

**40. Contrast between open and close o.** In M.E., there were two distinct kinds of *ō*, the one open, like the mod. E. *au* in *Paul* or *oa* in *broad* (an exceptional word which happens to preserve the old sound of M.E. *brŏŏd*), and the other close, like the mod. E. *o* in *note*, or the G. *o* in *so*. These sounds have usually passed into mod. E. *oa* in *road* and mod. E. *oo* in *cool* respectively, so that they are quite distinct even at this day. They are also easily distinguished by help of the A.S. sounds which originated them, and they may be denoted by writing *ŏŏ* for the *open* sound, and *oo* for the *close* one. In brŏad romic, the open *ō* may be written (ao), and the close *ō* as (oo). For example, M.E. *rŏŏd* (raod), riming with mod. E. *laud*, and now written *road* (roud), is quite distinct from M.E. *rood* (rood), riming with mod. E. *load*, and still written *rood*, but pronounced as (ruud), and riming with *food* (fuud) [1].

The M.E. open *ō* will be discussed first.

**41.** The M.E. open *ō* (ao) had two sources; it arose (1) from A.S. *ā*; or (2) from the lengthening of A.S. short *o* at the end of an open syllable. I have observed that Chaucer frequently makes a distinction between the open *ō* that arises from these two sources. The lengthened A.S. *o* produced a sound that was either a little shorter or a little closer than the other. We can distinguish them by writing (ŏŏ) for no. 1, and (ŏ) for no. 2 (above). Examples of (1) are A.S. *lāre*, dat. of *lār*, lore, whence M.E. *lore* (lŏŏ·rə) [2]; A.S. *māra*, more, whence M.E. *more* (mŏŏ·rə). Examples

---

[1] The forms printed between marks of parenthesis, such as (fuud), denote the pronunciation, according to the 'broad romic' notation, which is founded on the pronunciation of the Italian vowels. The preceding forms, printed in italics, such as *food*, denote the M.E. or modern E. spellings.

[2] The turned e (ə) represents the sound of the unaccented *a* in *China*. The raised stop (·) signifies that the accent falls on the preceding vowel.

of (2) are A.S. *forloren*, M.E. *forlore* (forlò·rə) ; A.S. *tōforan*,
M.E. *tofore* (toofò·rə\.

I now cite the instances in Part I of the Squieres Tale,
as exemplified in rimes.

(1) *Sore* (sòò·rə), a word of F. origin (from Late L.
*ex-aurare*), *more* (mòò·rə), from A.S. *māra*; 123. *Also*
(alsòò·), from A.S. *ealswā*, *foo* (fòò), from A.S. *fāh*; 135.
*Fro*, A.S. *frā*, *so*, A.S. *swā*; 189. *Knowe*, A.S. *cnāwan*,
*lowe*, from Icel. *lāgr*, adj.; 215. *Y-goon*, from A.S. *gān*,
*anoon*, from A.S. *on ān*; 293, 327. *Also*, from A.S. *ealswā*,
*tho*, A.S. *þā*; 307. *Two*, A.S. *twā*, *also*, A.S. *ealswā*; 317.

(2) *Therfore*, A.S. *þǣrfore* (dhèèrfò·rə), *bore*, A.S. *boren*;
177. *Y-swore*, A.S. *ge-sworen*, *y-bore*, A.S. *ge-boren*, 325.

**42.** The chief source of the M.E. close *ō* is the A.S. and
Icel. *ō*; as in A.S. *bōc*, M.E. *book* (book), a book, A.S. *dōm*,
M.E. *doom* (doom), doom. Examples are as follows. *Rote*,
from Icel. *rōt*, a root, *bōte*, from A.S. *bōt*, good, healing; 153.
*Sone*, A.S. *sōna*, soon, *done*, A.S. *dōnne*, to do; 333.

**43. Exceptions.** When we extend our investigations to
the whole of the Canterbury Tales, we find but few instances
of exceptional usage as regards the open *ō*. The exceptional
words are *mōre*, *before*, *therfore*. Of these, *mōre* rimes
once with the pp. *bore*, A 1541, and frequently with *before*.
*Before* rimes once with *mōre*, *lōre*, E 789; once with *sōre*,
D 631; once with *mōre*, *yōre*, E 65; once with *gōre*, A
3237, from A.S. *gār*. So also *therfore* (with the same suffix
*-fore*) once rimes with *yōre*, E 1140. With these few exceptions, we find the two sets in § 41 kept distinct. In
(1) we have *evermōre*, *namōre*, *mōre*, *lōre*, *hōre* (A.S. *hār*),
*gōre*, *ōre*, *rōre*, *sōre*, all with *ō* from A.S. *ā*; and in (2) we
have *before*, *bore*, *y-bore*, *forlore*, *swore*, *therfore*, *wherfore*, all
with a somewhat shorter or less sonorous *o* from A.S. *o*.

In spite of all the exceptional uses of the words *more* and
*before* (and *therfore*, once), we cannot but observe a remarkable tendency to keep asunder two vowel-sounds which it

required a delicate ear to distinguish.   It is interesting as
proving exceptional care on the part of the author.   It is
still more interesting to observe how little Lydgate and
others cared for such a distinction.

**44.** More important are the few exceptions in which the
close and open *ō* rime together.   This is very unusual ; and
Chaucer considered it as admissible in difficult cases only.

These cases are three.   The first is where *ō* is *final*, and
rimes are consequently scarce ; hence we find an exception
as to the very common word *do*.   M.E. *do* or *doon*, to do,
rimes *permissibly* with M.E. *go* or *goon* ; though *do* is from
A.S. *dōn*, and *go* from A.S. *gān*.   The other cases are also
those in which rimes are very scarce ; thus we find *dōm*,
doom, riming with *hōm*, home (B 3127), the A.S. forms
being *dōm*, *hām* ; but rimes in -*ōm* were so scarce that there
was little else to be done.   For the same reason *sothe*
(soo·dhə) rimes with *bothe* (bòò·dhə), in G 167.

With these three exceptions, the open and close *o* are
rigorously kept apart.

**45. Contrast between open and close e.**   This is
a more difficult matter, and is treated at length in the
six-volume edition, Introd. p. xxxv.   I here state the
results.

The M.E. open *ē* resulted from A.S. *ēa*, or from that
value of the A.S. *ǣ* which arose from mutation.   Thus the
A.S. *lēac*, a leek, gave M.E. *lèèk*, with open *e*, like *a* in
mod. E. *Mary* ; and the A.S. *hǣlan*, to heal, derived by
mutation from *hāl*, whole (Goth. *hails*\), gave M.E. *hèèlen*,
with open *e*.   Another open *e*, perhaps not quite so long,
arose from the lengthening of A.S. short *e* in an open
syllable.   Thus A.S. *brecan*, to break, gave M.E. *brèken*.
Observe that the M.E. open *ē* is usually written as *ea* in
modern English (*leek* being exceptional).

The M.E. close *ē* resulted from A.S. *ē* or *ēo*, as in M.E.
*swete*, from A.S. *swēte*, sweet ; M.E. *deep*, from A.S. *dēop*,

E

deep. This M.E. close *e* is usually written as *ee* in modern
English.

But there was a third variety of M.E. *ē* which seems to
have been intermediate between the other two; at any rate,
words containing it rime with *either* of the above vowels,
indifferently. This *ē* had two sources, viz. (1) A.S. *ǽ*, or
that variety of long *æ* which corresponds to the Gothic *ē*,
and arises from *gradation*, not by mutation[1]; and (2) A.S.
*īe*, later *ȳ*, Mercian *ē*, as in M.E. *ysēne*, visible, A.S. *gesīene*,
*gesȳne*, Mercian *gesēne*. This vowel, for the sake of distinct-
ness, may be called the 'neutral *ē*[2].' All that need be said
here is that, in considering Chaucer's rimes, it is simplest
to *exclude* all cases in which *ē* arises from the last two
sources. When this is done, we obtain the general rule,
that words containing the open *ē* never rime, in Chaucer,
with words containing the close *ē*. The only notable exception is that, owing to a paucity of rimes, the word *sèè*,
sea (A.S. *sǽ*, Goth. *saiws*) is allowed to rime with *see*, I see
(A.S. *sēo*); much as *do* rimes with *go* (§ 44). Such an
instance can also be set aside.

I now cite the instances of long *e* occurring in rime in
Part I of the Squiers Tale, with explanations; omitting
words of French origin.

Examples of open *ē* (from *ǽ* or *ēa*): *dèèd*, dead, *lustihèèd*,
287; and of open *ē* (resulting from lengthening of A.S. *e*):
*wère*, to wear, *bère*, to bear, 147; *spère*, spear, *dère*, to injure,

---

[1] The A.S. *ǽ* and *ǽ* (so marked in Sweet's A.S. Dict.) are easily
distinguished by help of comparative philology. The A.S. *ǽ* (*i*-muta-
tion of *ā*) answers to G. *ei*, Icel. *ei*, Goth. *ai*, as in A.S. *hǽlan*, to heal,
G. *heilen*, Icel. *heila*, Goth. *hailjan*; whereas A.S. *ǽ* (arising from
gradation) answers to G. *a*, Icel. *á*, Goth. *ē*, as in A.S. *wǽron*, were,
G. *waren*, Icel. *váru*, Goth. *wēsun*.

[2] Probably it is the same in quality as the 'half-open *e*' observed
in French. 'In pronunciation we can discriminate at least three
kinds of *e*: open *è* (as in *perte*), half-open *e* (as in *maison*), and close
*e* (as in *bonte*).'—Darmesteter, Hist. Fr. Grammar, § 23.

239. For an explanation of the lengthening of A.S. *e* in an open syllable, see my Primer of Eng. Etymology, § 30.

Examples of close *ē*: *be, ye,* 1 ; *semed, demed,* 201 ; *been, be, are, been,* bees, 203 ; *be, me,* 245.

Examples of neutral *ē* (marked *ê*) riming with open *ē*: *wêre,* were, *êre,* ear, 195 ; *anywhêre, êre,* 315.

Examples of neutral *ē* (marked *ê*) riming with close *ē*: *shêne, grene,* 53 ; *here,* here, *hêre,* to hear, 145.

Examples of neutral *ē* riming together : *rêde, drêde,* 211 ; *hêre,* to hear, *dêre,* dear, 271.

46. I now give lists of words, for convenience of reference.

An investigation of all the rimes containing *ē* and *ō* in the Canterbury Tales gives the following results.

Words containing these vowels are arranged below in two sets. In those marked (A) the *ē* or *ō* was open; and in those marked (B) the *ē* or *ō* was close.

RULE. Words in the list (A) rime with one another, but never with those in (B). Words in the list (B) rime with one another, but never with those in (A). I also give a list (C), containing words with neutral *ē*, which rime with either those in (A) or those in (B).

It may be remarked that these facts are incontrovertible and *remain true,* even if the above explanations are all wrong. Hence they can be depended upon as tests.

And it is most essential to observe that any one, however ignorant of Middle English phonology, can *verify* the results here given in a few minutes, by simple reference to Mr. Cromie's Rime-Index to the Canterbury Tales[1]; and the A.S. forms can be verified by help of my Concise Etymological Dictionary. There is no mode of wriggling

---

[1] Only there should also be ultimate reference to the text itself. Mr. Cromie sometimes misspells words; thus he has 'sheepe' for 'sheep,' Prol. 504. This is because the Ellesmere MS. has a senseless flourish after the *p,* misrepresented in the six-text edition by printing 'sheep*e*,' with idle *e.*

away from the conclusions, nor any room for denying them. Even the unlearned can note the difference in spelling (in many cases) between the mod. E. *ea* and *ee*.

**-eche.** (A) *tèche*, to teach, *bitèche*. (B) *seche*, to seek, *biseche*, to beseech. (C) *eche*, to eke, *leche*, *speche*; to which add *preche*, of F. origin.

**-ede.** (A) *brède*, breadth, *dède*, dead, *hède*, head, *lède*, lead (a metal), *rède*, red[1], *sprède*, to spread; so also *mede*, a meadow, *wede*, clothing, though belonging etymologically to (C). (B) *bede*, to offer, *blede*, to bleed, *crede*, creed, *fede*, feed, *forbede*, *glede*, gleed, *mede*, reward, *nede*[2], need, *spede*, to speed, *stede*, a steed. (C) *dede*, deed, *drede*, s. and v., *hede*, to heed, *rede*, to advise. Words in *-hede*, -hood, almost always show open *e*, but a few exceptions occur, as in E 883, 1075.

**-edeth.** (B) *bedeth*, offers, *bredeth*, breeds; E 1783.

**-eed.** (A) *brèèd*, bread, *dèèd*, dead, *hèèd*, head, *lèèd*, lead, *rèèd*, red, *thrèèd*, thread. (C) *heed*, heed, *reed*, counsel, *seed*, seed.

**-eef.** (A) *dèèf*, deaf, *lèèf*, leaf. (B) *leef*, lief, *theef*, thief; and the French words *preef*, proof, *mischeef*, mischief.

But in A 1837, owing to the identity of the initial *l*, we find *leef*, lief, riming with *lèèf*, a leaf; by a poetical licence.

**-eem.** (A) *bèèm*, *drèèm*, *strèèm*.

**-eme.** (B) *deme*, deem; *seme*, seem.

**-een.** (B) *been*, bees, *been*, are, *seen*, see, *streen*, stock.

**-eke.** (A) *brèke*, to break, *spèke*, to speak, *wrèke*, to wreak, *awrèke*, *ywrèke*, with original short *e*; *lèke*, a leek. (B) *meke*, meek, *seke*, to seek, *biseke*, to beseech, *seke*, sick. (C) *cheke*, cheek. Also *eke*, eek, usually has close *ē*, as if belonging to (B); but it once rimes with *spèke*, H 324.

**-ele.** (A) *hèle*, to hide, *mèle*, meal of corn, *stèle*, a handle;

---

[1] Formerly *read*; still spelt *Read*, as a proper name.
[2] *Nede*, from A.S. *nēod*. It once occurs as *nèèd* (cf. A.S. *nīed*), riming with *hèèd*, head, Bk. Duch. 1253.

with original short *e* ; *dèle*, to deal, *hèle*, health.    (B) *fele*, to
feel, *hele*, heel, *knele*, kneel.

**-ene.**    (A) *bène*, bean, *clène*, clean, *lène*, lean, *mène*, to
mean, *unclène*, unclean.    (B) *bitwene*, between, *grene*, green,
*kene*, keen, *quene*, queen, *sene*, to see, *tene*, teen (vexation),
*wene*, to ween.    (C) *sene*, *y-sene*, adj., visible, *shene*, bright.

**-epe.**    (A) *chèpe*, to buy (cf. E. cheap), *hèpe*, to heap,
*lèpe*, to leap, *stèpe*, bright, *thrèpe*, to call ; also *clèpe*, to call
(orig. with short *e*).    (B) *crepe*, to creep, *depe*, deep, *kepe*, to
keep, *wepe*, to weep.    (C) *slepe*, to sleep.

**-ere.**    (A) *answère*, sb., an answer, *bère*, a bear, *bère*
(A.S. *beran*), to bear, *dère* (A.S. *derian*), to harm, *ère*, to ear
(plough), *hère*, her, *spère*, a spear, *stère*, to stir, *swère*, to
swear, *tère*, to tear, *wère*, to defend, *wère*, to wear ; all from
A.S. short *e* (or *i*) ; also *ère*, ear, *gère*, gear, *tère*, a tear.
Also usually *there*, there, *were*, were, *where*, where ; though
belonging to  C) by etymology.    (B) *fere*, feer (companion),
*here*, here, *yfere*, together.    Here belong the French words
*appere*, appear, *chere*, cheer, *clere*, clear, *frere*, friar, *manére*,
manner, *matére*, matter, *spere*, sphere.    (C) *bere*, bier (A.S.
*bèèr*), *dere*, dear, *fere*, fear, *here*, to hear, *lere*, to teach (which
should belong to the *first* set), *yere*, year [1].

**-eres.**    (A) *ères*, ears, *shères*, shears, *tères*, tears.    Also
(from A.S. short *e*) *bères*, bears, *hoppestères*, *fruitestères*,
*tombestères*.    (B) *courseres*, *freres*, *officeres*, *preyeres*, *squieres*,
*wafereres* ; all of French origin.    (C) *breres*, briars, *geres*,
whims, *heres*, hairs (cf. G. *haar*), *yeres*, years.

---

[1] Mr. Cromie has a curious error at p. 108.    He says that, in
A 1421, *here* (adverb, here) rimes with *bere* (verb, to bear).    This is
impossible ; and in fact *here* is not an adverb, but the fem. pers.
pronoun, meaning 'her.'    *Here* (her) occurs again elsewhere ; it
rimes with *bere*, a bear, *bere*, to bear, *swere*, to swear, *were*, to wear,
and *spere*, a spear ; all with *e* = A.S. short *e*.    So again, at p. 89, he
explains *stele* by ' steel ' ; but, when it rimes with *hele*, to hide, and
*stele*, to steal, the *e* is obviously short, and it must mean ' a handle.'
And so it does ; see A 3785, D 949.

It is remarkable that the ending *-ere*, pl. *-eres*, had the open *e* in words of native origin, but the close *e* in words of French origin; cf. ten Brink, § 67 (γ). This explains why, in C 477–480, four lines which *appear* to rime together really form distinct pairs; the final words being *tombestères*, *fruitestères* (from the A.S. suffix *-estre*), and *waferéres*, *officéres* (of French origin).

**-ete.** (A) *bète*, to beat, *grète*, great, *hète*, heat, *swète*, to sweat, *wète*, wet, *whète*, wheat, *ybète*, beaten. Also *ète*, to eat, *mète*, meat; from A.S. *etan*, *mete*. (B) *bete*, to mend[1], *flete*, to float, *swete*, sweet. (C) *bihete*, to promise, *lete*, to let, *forlete*, to let go, *shete*, a sheet, *strete*, a street.

**-eve.** (A) *birève*, to bereave, *dève*, pl. deaf, *grève*, a grove (in the pl. *grèves*), *rève*, to reave. (B) *leve*, lief, dear, *reve*, a reeve. (C) *eve*, eve, *leve*, to believe, *leve*, to permit, *bileve*, belief. Note that *yeve*, to give, usually rimes with *live*, to live, as in mod. English.

**-o.** *All* words in *-ō* are allowed to rime together. Of these, *to*, *therto*, *unto*, *do*, *fordo*, had the close sound.

**-olde.** *Nolde*, *sholde*, *wolde*, usually rime together; sometimes *wolde* rimes with other words, as *holde*, *olde*, *tolde*.

**-one.** (A) *alone*, *echone*, each one, *grone*, to groan, *lone*, loan, *mone*, to moan. (B) *bone*, boon, *eftsone*, eft-soon, *mone*, moon, *sone*, soon. Note how mod. E. distinguishes the sounds. Observe that *sone*, son[2], *wone*, to dwell, are really written for *sune*, *wune*, and rime with each other only.

**-onge.** Note that *songe*, pp., *spronge*, pp., *tonge*, *yonge*,

[1] A proper understanding of these rimes is a guide to the meaning of words. Mr. Cromie, at p. 85, says that *bete* means 'to beat'; but, when it rimes with *shete*, to shoot, and *swete*, sweet, it means 'to mend,' from A.S *bētan*; see A 2253, 3927. *Beat* is from A.S. *bēatan*.

[2] At p. 176, Mr. Cromie explains *sone* by 'sun'; it is merely a misprint for 'son.' At p. 178, he has *sonne*, also explained by 'sun'; correctly.

*ystonge*, are really written for *sunge*, *sprunge*, *tunge*, *yunge*, *ystunge*, and rime together. But they are quite distinct from *fonge*, *honge*, *longe*, *stronge*, *wronge*; as in modern English.

**-ood.** (A) *abood*, abode, *bood*, bode, *bistrood*, bestrode, *brood*, broad, *glood*, glode (did glide), *hood*, suffix (A.S. *-hād*). (B) *blood*, *flood*, *good*, *hood*, *mood*, *stood*, *understood*, *wood* (mad).

**-ook.** (A) *ook*, an oak, *strook*, a stroke. (B) *awook* (A.S. *onwōc*), *book*, *cook*, *forsook*, *hook*, *quook*, *shook*, *took*, *wook*.

**-oot.** (A) *boot*, boat, *boot*, he bit, *goot*, goat, *hoot*, hot, *noot*, know not, *smoot*, smote, *woot*, know, *wroot*, wrote. (B) [*foot*, *moot*, must, *soot*; in Troilus].

**-ooth.** (A) *clooth*, *gooth*, goes, *looth*, *ooth*, *wrooth*. (B) *dooth*, *sooth*, *tooth*.

**-ore.** *Bifore*, *bore*, pp., born, *forlore*, pp., *swore*, pp., *therfore*, *wherfore*, had originally a short *o*, and so usually rime together; and rarely with *sōre* (from A.S. *sār*), &c. Exceptions in the C. T. are due to *bifore*, before, which frequently rimes with *mōre*, &c.; and to the rimes *mōre*, *bore*, A 1541; *yōre*, *therfore*, E 1140.

**-ote.** (A) *grote*, groat, *hote*, hot, *throte*, throat. (B) *bote*, boot (satisfaction), *fote*, foot, *rote*, root, *swote* or *soote* or *sote*, sweet. Observe that when *rote* rimes with an open *o*, as e. g. with *cote*, a coat, A 327, or *note*, a note, A 235, B 1711, or *throte*, throat, B 1735, it must itself have an open *o*. In such cases, it no longer means 'root,' but either occurs in the phrase *by rote*, or denotes a musical instrument. A fact like this is extremely instructive.

# CHAPTER V

**47.** In the preceding chapters we have obtained sufficient positive evidence as to Chaucer's habits of grammatical
usage and rime. These have been obtained from a survey of
the Canterbury Tales, and from an analysis of Part I of the
Squieres Tale in particular. It is obvious that such a knowledge of his habits will be very helpful in considering
internal evidence. But it will be well to take the external
evidence first.

**48.** The postulate with which we started was that
Chaucer was the author of the Canterbury Tales. From
this a good deal more easily follows.

The author of the Canterbury Tales, naming himself
Chaucer, especially claims to have written the Legend of
Good Women (B 47-76). Again, the author of the latter
claims to have translated the Romaunt of the Rose, and
to have written Troilus, The Hous of Fame, The Book of
the Duchesse, The Parliament of Foules, a prose translation
of Boethius, The Life of St. Cecilia (i.e. the Seconde.
Nonnes Tale), and various Balades, Roundels, and Virelays.
Lydgate bears similar testimony, adding Anelida and
Arcite and the Complaint of Mars. All these (except the
Romaunt) are undisputed, and we thus at once add to
the Canterbury Tales the following, viz. 1. The Legend

of Good Women ; 2. Troilus ; 3. The Hous of Fame ;
4. a prose translation of Boethius ; 5. The Parliament of
Foules ; 6. The Book of the Duchesse ; 7. Anelida and
Arcite ; 8. The Complaint of Mars.   Before going further,
let us see how these fall into line with the Canterbury
Tales.   Is the *internal* evidence in their favour consistent
with the external evidence in favour of their genuineness ?

**49. The Legend of Good Women.**   This is closely
linked to the Canterbury Tales by the peculiarity of its
metre.   It was here (or in the Knightes Tale) that Chaucer
first developed the capabilities of the five-stressed riming
couplet.   He saw at once how convenient it was for a
poem of considerable length, and adopted it as the main
metre of the Tales also.   All other English poems written
in this metre are later than 1400.

We must next consider the grammatical forms.   How
do they agree with the rules given in Chapter III ?

Suppose we examine the Legend of Tisbee, consisting
of 218 lines.   We must first of all see if there is any grave
difference between the texts in S. and G.

With a few trifling differences of reading, not affecting
the scansion, the texts are identical, except in a few
details of spelling.   As before, the text in G. is one in
which the 'idle' -*e* is frequently retained, with a warning
at the same time that it does not count.   That is, we have
*There* for *Ther*, *hire* for *hir*, *lykynge* for *lyking*, &c.   Sad
to say, some of these spellings are downright blunders ; it
is astonishing to find *ranne* for *ran*, *tooke* for *took*, *sytte* for
*sit* (she sits), *come* for *com* (he came), *founde* for *found*,
*slayne* for *slayn*, *torne* for *torn*, *uppe* for *up*, and the like.
It would hardly be thought advisable in modern German
to express *he ran* by *er ranne*, or *he found* by *er fande*, or
'up' by *auffe*.   Against such singular vagaries the reader
may well be warned.   He can then consult either S. or G.,
as is most convenient.

And now for the twenty-two grammatical tests in Chap. IV.

**50. Final -es**; see § 28 (1, 2, 3). I only observe one genitive case, but it is correct, viz. *lov-es*, 914. As to plurals in *-es*, there are three examples, *wall-es, tyl-es, lord-es*, in the first six lines, and the reader may find about twenty more for himself. Just as in the C. T., the plural ends in *-s* only, when the accent is thrown back; e. g. *máyden-s*, 722, *wárdeyn-s*, 753, *lóver-s*, 743. The pl. *ydól-es*, idols, 786, is worth notice. As for the adv. in *-es*, see *on-es*, 760, 761.

**Final -en**; see § 29 (4, 5, 6, 7, 8). Examples of No. 4 (infin.): dichen, 708, fallen, 758, 839, kissen, 761, renden (or renten), 843, holden, 857, espyen, 858, tellen, 860, fol(o)wen, 894.

Examples of no. 5 (gerund): to trusten, 801, to drinken, 808.

Examples of no. 6 (pp.); clov*en*, 738; graven, 785, broken, 852, comen, 856.

Examples of no. 7 (pr. pl.): we prayen, 902, we moten, 903; (pt. pl.) woneden, 712, diden, 723, speken, 734, founden, 744, weren, 767, 901, wolden, 768, 769, plighten, 778, useden, 787.

Example of no. 8 (prep.): withouten, 866.

**Final -e**; see §§ 31 (9-12), 32 (13-16), 33 (17-22). The student should investigate the examples for himself; he will find the exercise instructive. I give only *one* example in each case, the first that I observe. These are: no. 9, wone, 714;—no. 10, doute, 721;—no. 11, grave, dat., 788;—no. 12 (no example);—no. 13, the lustieste, 716;—no. 14, this noble, 710;—no. 15, harde, 709;—no. 16, grene (used as sb.), 712;—no. 17, make, 708;—no. 18, to receyve, 752;—no. 19, y-bake, 709;—no. 20, brente, 731;—no. 21, falle, pr. s. subj., 855;—no. 22, bitwene, prep. 713. But the student should make a thorough analysis of the legend, by parsing every word of it; he would then realise how intimately the grammar and the scansion are bound up together, and how nearly every little peculiarity observable in the Squieres Tale reappears in The Legend of Thisbe. Thus the extra syllable at the cæsura is clearly seen in l. 772 :—And long-e tym-e | they wroght' in this manére.

**51. Rime-tests.** In §§ 37–46 above, various Rime-tests have been noted. It will be found, of course, that they are all fairly enough recognised in The Legend of Thisbe. I here give the results.

Test in § 38 : rimes in *-y* as distinct from *-ye* : prevely, subtilly, 796; only, trewely, 896. Also : jelosy-e, foly-e, 722 ; espy-e, ly-e, 742 ; envy-e, ly-e, 902.

Test in § 39 : rimes in *-ight(e)* as distinct from *-yt(e)* : lyte, myte, 740; nighte, mighte, 838.

Test in §§ 40–44 : contrast between open $\bar{o}$ and close $\bar{o}$. Instances of open $\bar{o}$ are these : wo, so, 748 ; two, so, 758 ; ago, mo, 916 ; goon, stoon, 764, 768 ; everichoon, goon, 780 ; sore, more, 846 ; agroos, aroos, 830 ; gost, bost, 886 ; hoot, smoot, 914 ; throwe, knowe, 866. Instances of close $\bar{o}$ are these : wood (mad), stood, 736.

In the following words, *o* denotes short *u* (as in E. *full*) : wone, sone, 714 ; y-shove, love, 726 ; nome, come, 822 [1].

Test in §§ 45, 46 : contrast between open $\bar{e}$ and close $\bar{e}$. Instances of open $\bar{e}$ are these : thrète, y-bète, 754 ; hète, wète, 774 ; hèèd, dèèd, 882 ; shèthe, dèthe, 888. Instances of close $\bar{e}$ are these : be, tree, 784; see, be, 794 : he, y-see, 824 ; be, ye, 840 ; she, me, 890 ; be, she, 894 ; me, thee, 898 ; grene, bitwene, 712 ; mete (to meet), swete (sweet), 760. In drêde, dêde, 860, both vowels are of the neutral character.

There is no difficulty as to the rimes in this Legend.

---

[1] The A.F. scribes often wrote *o* for short *u* before or after the symbols *m*, *n*, or *u* (for *v*). This is why we still absurdly write *monk* (but not *stonk*); *come* (but not *domb*); whilst *dove* differs from *rove* and *move*.

**52.** In precisely the same way we might take any passage in Troilus, and show that it satisfies, to a reasonable degree, all the grammatical usages and all the rime-tests. Indeed, the complete history of the rime-tests as to the open and close *o* and open and close *e* came out of an analysis which I formerly made of all the rimes in Troilus; see my Rime-Index to Troilus, published for the Chaucer Society in 1891.

Similar internal evidence is completely satisfactory as to the other poems mentioned above in § 48, viz. The Hous of Fame, The Parliament of Foules, The Book of the Duchesse, Anelida and Arcite, and The Complaint of Mars. As all these are admittedly Chaucer's, we need say no more about them here.

**53.** Further external testimony is attainable from the MS. collections made by John Shirley (see six-vol. ed., i. 25) and from the notes made by scribes in various MSS., especially MSS. Fairfax 16, Pepys 2006, and those in the Cambridge University Library marked Ii. 3. 21 and Hh. 4. 12 (see six-vol. ed., i. 25, 26). In this way we are entitled to assign to Chaucer the following Minor Poems, in addition to those already mentioned (I follow the order in S.): An ABC; The Compleynte unto Pite; a Compleint to his Lady[1]; Chaucers Wordes unto Adam; The Former Age; Fortune; To Rosemounde; Truth; Gentilesse; Lak of Stedfastnesse; Lenvoy de Chaucer a Scogan; Lenvoy de Chaucer a Bukton; The Compleynt of Venus; The Compleint of Chaucer to his empty Purse; Proverbs (8 lines only). As none of these are disputed, I will only say that they all satisfy, as well as might be expected, the rules above given as to grammar and rime. Though written at various times, some of them being separated from others by considerable intervals, they

---

[1] I pronounced in favour of the genuineness of this poem *before* the discovery of the ascription of it to Chaucer in MS. Phillipps 9053.

exhibit a consistent and hardly variable treatment. The tests that apply to the Canterbury Tales can be applied to them all, without eliciting any important anomaly [1]. The reader can satisfy himself that such is the case by making an analysis of any one of them that he suspects. I have shown above how this can be done.

We have also MS. authority for assigning to Chaucer the (unfinished) Treatise on the Astrolabe, the authenticity of which is not doubted [2]; in fact, the Canterbury Tales show that Chaucer was certainly a student of astronomy.

**54.** All the Poems printed in S. and G. have now been mentioned, except the following comparatively unimportant ones [3]. Merciless Beauty; Balade against Women Inconstant; Compleint Damours; A Balade of Compleynt; Womanly Noblesse.

A few words as to each of these may be of service.

**Merciless Beauty.** First printed as an 'Original Ballad by Chaucer' in Percy's 'Reliques of Ancient English Poetry'; though it is not a ballad, but a triple roundel. There is *some* external evidence in its favour. It occurs in a Chaucer-Lydgate MS., where it is the last poem in the MS. and is preceded by *nine* Chaucerian poems; and it is clearly not Lydgate's. It was doubtless for this reason that Percy took it to be Chaucer's. Chaucer wrote roundels, and this is a most perfect specimen of a triple roundel. It was once well known, as the first line of it is quoted by Lydgate (see Chaucerian Poems, p. 281, l. 21). The internal evidence in its favour is very strong.

---

[1] In the ' Proverbs,' l. 7, the infin. *embrac-e* is shortened to *embrac'*, to rime with *compas* ; which the popular form of the metre allows. But the whole poem contains only eight lines, and is of trifling value.

[2] Except a few sections at the end. Part I and Part II, sections 1–40, are admittedly genuine.

[3] There are difficulties as to The Romaunt of the Rose. It is fully discussed below, in Chapters vi–viii.

Every final -es, -en, and -e is correctly used. In the course of only twenty-four (independent) lines, we find a plural in -es (35), a genitive in -es (5)[1], and an infin. in -en (4); whilst the final -e constitutes a syllable about twenty times; twice in a gerund (15, 18); thrice in an infinitive (2, 22, 30); in the sbs. *herte* (3, 14), *wounde* (5), *quene* (9), *trouthe* (10), *bene* (29), *mene* (36); in the French sbs. *cheyne* (16), *peyne* (23); in the adjectives *kene* (3), *grene* (5), *sene* (10), *lene* (28); in the present indicative *mene* (31), and in the subjunctive *sterve* (23). But the most surprising point is the careful distinction between the open and close $\bar{e}$ and the diphthong *ey* in the rimes. The first roundel has rimes on close $\bar{e}$, the second on *ey*, and the third on open $\bar{e}$; in all cases followed by the suffix -ne. When the general excellence of these roundels is also taken into consideration, the case in its favour is a very strong one.

**55. Balade against Women Unconstant.** There is some external evidence in its favour. In MS. Cleop. D. 7, we find four short poems together in the same hand; of these, three are Chaucer's, and this Balade comes last. In MS. Harl. 7578, three poems are found together; of these, two are Chaucer's, and this Balade follows them. In both MSS. it is accompanied by Chaucer's Gentilesse and Lak of Stedfastnesse, in the same metre. Further, the general idea of the poem, and the whole of the refrain, are taken from Chaucer's favourite author Machault, whose refrain is—'En lieu de bleu, Damë, vous vestez vert.' It has not been shown that any one but Chaucer was acquainted with Machault.

In Stowe's edition of 1561, the title is—'A balade which Chaucer made agaynst women vnconstaunt.' But we do not know what authority Stowe had for this.

The internal evidence is satisfactory. Such contractions

---

[1] *Hertes* occurs again in Compl. of Mars, 57; still, I think it should be *herte*, as in other places. This does not affect the scansion.

as *com'th*, *far'th*, *turn'th*, for *cometh*, *fareth*, *turneth*, are common enough in Chaucer.

The chief point against it is the use of *mene*, in l. 20, riming with *kene*, *grene* (with close *ē*) and *sene* (with neutral *ē*); for the *e* in *mene* should be open, as the derivation is from A.S. *mǣnan*. Still, this is not fatal, as Chaucer certainly has *lere*, to teach, from A.S. *lǣran*, riming with *here*, here, from A.S. *hēr*, with close *-ē*; C. T., G 607. The difference between the A.S. *ǣ*, arising from mutation, and the A.S. *ǣ*, arising from gradation, is usually observed, but this fine distinction sometimes fails; in fact, Gower rimes *mene* with *quéne* and *wéne*; C. A. i. 210, 308.

I see no adequate reason for rejecting this piece from the Canon of his works.

**56. Compleynt Damours.** Here external evidence fails, as is the case with the other Minor Poems that follow, with the exception of Womanly Noblesse.

The internal evidence is in its favour, in as far as it conforms to the grammatical rules. The rimes are all perfect. There are five lines ending in *-yë*, none in *-y*. The open and close *ō* are kept apart, except in the case of *do*, *wo*, *go* (16); a common exception, as shown in § 44. The open and close *ē* are likewise kept apart. It is not a poem of much merit, still it is not certainly spurious. It is of some value as affording a good specimen of a 'Complaint.'

I think it may be retained among the *doubtful* poems.

**57. A Balade of Compleynt.** I drew attention to this, as being a fair sample of a short Complaint. There is no external evidence in its favour.

*Compleyne* in l. 1 should rather be *compleyn-e*, against the scansion; and similarly *presénce* in l. 3 should be *presénc-è*.

The rime *in-fere* (with close *ē*) and *were* (almost always with open *ē*) raises a difficulty.

With one exception (viz. *hert-e* in l. 1) every final *-e* that does not occur in rime is either elided or comes at the caesura. My present belief is that it is probably by Lydgate. Compare ll. 13, 14 with the Temple of Glas, 1196, and l. 17 with the same, 1015. I now think it should certainly be excluded from the list of Chaucer's poems.

**58. Womanly Noblesse.** In this case we have external evidence, as it is headed 'Balade that Chaucier made,' the ascription being by Shirley, who (as far as can be traced) is invariably right as to Chaucer's poems.

A strong point in its favour is the uniqueness of its metre. I know of no other poem with only three rimes in thirty-three lines, with the lines similarly arranged. The 9-line stanza ($a\,a\,b\,a\,a\,b\,b\,a\,b$) occurs again only in Anelida and Arcite (211–255, 281–316), and the Envoy ($a\,c\,a\,c\,a\,a$) is unique. Nine of the riming words are the same as in Anelida. Considering that Chaucer was an experimentalist in metre, whilst Occleve and Lydgate did no more than copy him, and originated nothing in this direction, we are bound to accept the poem as genuine. Indeed, I can see no reason why it should be branded as 'doubtful.'

**59.** In the six-volume edition, vol. iv. pp. xxvii and xxix, I printed two Complaints which are quite in Chaucer's manner, viz. A Complaint to my Mortal Foe, and a Complaint to my Lode-star. As these fairly recognise his rules for grammar and rime, I was inclined to place them in the category of doubtful poems ; and, indeed, they have a far stronger claim than poems which set all Chaucer's usages at utter defiance. It would appear, however, from some of the stanzas in The Black Knight and in The Temple of Glass, that Lydgate, before he grew careless in his metre, might have achieved poems as good as these seem to be. The question can very well wait till we have further light.

# CHAPTER VI

## THE ROMAUNT OF THE ROSE: FRAGMENT A

60. THE case of The Romaunt of the Rose is peculiar, and deserves three chapters to itself.

The difficulty arises from the fact that it is not homogeneous, but consists of *three* distinct parts. It was long before this was discovered; and of course it was possible, *before* this discovery, to obtain variable results by analysing different parts of it. Following up some hints given by Mr. Bradshaw, I showed, as far back as 1880, that it presented insuperable difficulties, and so came to the conclusion that it is not genuine; a result which, after all, is correct as regards the greater part of it.

But it was shown by Lindner, in 1888, that the poem was separable into two distinct parts; and further, not long afterwards, by Kaluza, that the number of these parts is rather three than two. It often happens that such theories have not much foundation; but in the present case, the distinction of the poems into three Fragments is so clear, when once pointed out, that there is no possibility of mistake. As this fortunately admits of a high degree of proof, the results will be stated, and the reasons for them sufficiently indicated.

To save time, and for the sake of clearness, let us call the French original *Le Roman*, and the English version *The Romaunt*. *Le Roman* is of portentous length, extending, in Méon's edition, to 22,074 lines. But The Romaunt

F

is imperfect, as it translates only ll. 1–5169, and 10716–12564, thus at once presenting two distinct Fragments, with a large gap between them. But it further appears that the former of these Fragments is by two hands, a fact which increases their real number to three; and it is convenient to denote these Fragments by the letters A, B, and C. The arrangement then stands thus :—

Fragment A.—Lines 1–1705. French text, 1–1678.

Fragment B.—Lines 1706–5810. French text, 1679–5169.

Fragment C.—Lines 5811–7678. French text, 10716–12564.

**61. Fragment A** (1–1705). There is no real difficulty in accepting this Fragment as genuine; and as we know that Chaucer actually made a translation of *Le Roman*, of which he displays in his works an intimate knowledge, we may as well at once accept it. There are two false rimes, viz. at ll. 505 and 1341; but in both places there is clearly some corruption in the text; see my Notes on these passages. Otherwise, all the grammatical and rime-tests are sufficiently satisfied. It will suffice to note some of the most striking results.

Final *-es* marks the gen. sing., as in *lord-es*, 1250; the plural of sbs., as in *drem-es*, 8; or an adverbial ending, as in *cert-es*, 439, 651, 689. Cf. § 28 (1, 2, 3).

Final *-en* marks the infinitive, as in *wax-en*, 53; the gerund, as in *to preis-en*, 70; the strong pp., as in *bigonn-en*, 43; the pres. pl., as in *drem-en*, 18; or a preposition, as in *without-en*, 1588. Cf. § 29 (4, 5, 6, 7, 8).

Final *-e* marks the nom. case, as in *nos-e*, 157; the acc. case of a French sb., as in *heritag-e*, 201; the dative, as in *bleyn-e*, 553; the genitive, as in *hert-e*, 1662; and perhaps in *mon-e-light*, 1010 (if *mone* here represents the A.S. *mōnan*). Cf. § 31 (9, 10, 11, 12).

In adjectives, it marks the definite form, as in *the lass-e*,

187; forms of French origin, as *fad-e*, 311; the plural, as in *yong-e*, 82; or a form that is etymologically dissyllabic, as *new-e*, 64; *soft-e*, 128. Cf. § 32 (13, 14, 15, 16).

In verbs, it marks the infinitive, as in *draw-e*, 6; the gerund, as in *to mak-e*, 79; the strong pp., as in *found-e*, 626; the weak pt. t., as in *went-e*, 23; the pr. s. subj., as in *ask-e*, 35; an adverb, as in *therinn-e*, 506; or a preposition, as in *without-e*, 553. Cf. § 33 (17, 18, 19, 20, 21), and § 34 (22).

Observe, lastly, adverbs such as *queynt-e-ly*, 783. Cf. § 34 (23).

**62.** The above examples are mere specimens; of course the true force of their significance lies in the fact that the grammatical rules are observed not merely here and there, but (for the most part) throughout. The examples given above are all taken from words that occur elsewhere than at the end of the line, because such examples are more obvious to the ordinary reader; nevertheless, it is most important (indeed, vital to the argument) to observe that the rules are most strictly observed in riming words, without any material exception. It is possible to find examples in which the final *-e* (or *-es*, or *-en*) may be neglected in the middle of a verse; but never at the end, where there is plenty of time for utterance. Thus the pl. form of *glad* is *glad-e*, but the final *-e* is of small value at the cæsura in l. 75 :—

'So glád-e ‖ that théy shew*e* ín singíng.'

And, in the same line, the final *-e* of *shew-e* is, of course, elided.

But the riming words can always be depended on, not only throughout the Canterbury Tales, but everywhere else in the genuine works of Chaucer, for yielding trustworthy grammatical results. It is for this reason that those who are interested in claiming pieces as genuine which Chaucer never wrote are especially impatient of rime-tests; for the unerring certainty with which they can be applied is obviously and distressingly inconvenient. The best-sustained attack upon the accuracy of Chaucer's rimes is that by Professor Lounsbury, in his (otherwise) admirable book entitled Studies of Chaucer, a work which no Chaucerian student can afford to neglect. Nearly all his objections have been met in my General Introduction to Chaucer's Works, vol. vi. pp. l–lvi ; and have been shown to arise from a misunderstanding of the grammatical usages of the time. After all the objections have been fairly considered, it turns out that, in the whole of the Canterbury Tales, there is ONLY ONE INSTANCE [1] in which strict grammar appears to be violated, viz. in Group F 1273 :—

'His tables Tolletanes forth he brought,
Ful wel corrected, ne there lakked nought
Neither his cóllect ne his expans yeres.'

Here it is quite clear that *brought* should have been *brought-e* (dissyllabic), as in A.S. *bröhte*, past tense singular ; and the mistake might easily have been avoided by writing *were* for *he*. We may therefore suspect that the mistake lies *in the other line*; and indeed, there is reason for supposing that the right reading is *nought-e*, dat., meaning 'in no respect'; used in the same way as A.S. *nähte* [2]. Still, even if it could be proved that, in the course of 17,385 lines, Chaucer once sinned against the exact usages of a grammar which was fast becoming obsolete, it is surely absurd to conclude, from a single example, that he *therefore* wrote The Flower and the Leaf, in which

---

[1] That is to say, only one probable instance is alleged. But there is really another instance of the same kind in C. T., A 4117, where *nought* (or *noughte*), meaning 'in no way,' rimes with *bisought-e*, pt. t. pl., they besought.

[2] Cf. 'ne bïð nähte wurð,' shall be nothing worth ; Ælfric, Lives of the Saints, xxi. 55 ; 'nöhte ðon mä,' not any the more, Gregory's Pastoral Care, p. 163, l. 19.

(in addition to a large number of other anomalies) we
find the pt. t. *might-e* riming with *wight* (18, 69, 312),
the pt. t. *wrought-e* with the pp. *y-wrought* (49), the pt. t.
*might-e* with *right* (299), and with *night* (588); i. e. six
anomalies in the course of 595 lines. There is such
a thing as a sense of proportion.

**63.** But Fragment A of The Romaunt is, in this respect,
immaculate. To save space, I only give the references.
Here follow references (1) for the weak pt. t., always with
final -*e* (or -*en*); and (2) for the weak pp., in which the final
-*e* is absent.

(1) 246[1], 250, 367[2], 452, 499, 587[3], 673, 701, 745[4], 851,
875, 1007, 1021, 1071, 1149, 1158, 1218, 1247[5], 1285,
1291, 1331, 1477, 1489[6], 1515, 1669, 1671[7].

(2) 61[8], 86, 329, 427, 471[9], 483, 603[10], 836, 846, 907[11],
941, 1163, 1193, 1227[12], 1397[12], 1419, 1436, 1533, 1657.

In no case does the weak pt. t. rime with the weak pp.,
as in The Flower and the Leaf, 49.

In the same way, any other form in -*e* can be tested.
I here give some references for the infinitive mood, as
exemplified in the rimes. They are: 14, 38, 87, 95, 110,
147, 176, 194, 252, 255, 279, 346, &c.; all of which are
correctly written, even in the MS.

And here are some gerunds: 24, 41, 58, 101, 158, 190,
280, 344, 345, &c.

**64.** Not to labour this point over much, let us apply

---

[1] G. has *went*, error for *wente*; we must pay no attention to the
printed form, as G. follows the careless MS.; we have only to deal
with *the spoken form*, which in Chaucer's English was *went-e*, as in
A.S.       [2] See note 1; for *potent-e*, see Troil. v. 1222.       [3] G. *myght*,
*hight*; read *mighte, highte*.       [4] Read *highte, lighte*; the *light-e* is the
definite form.       [5] Read *highte, highte* (dative).       [6] Or read *deyde*,
*preyde*.       [7] Read *forthoughte, wroughte*.       [8] Read *forget* (contracted
3 p. s. present), *set*.       [9] Read *fed, cled*.       [10] Either read *fet, set*,
sing.; or *fette, y-sette*, plural.       [11] Read *set*, as in 846.       [12] Read
*bistad, adrad*.       [13] Read *knet, set*.

a test of somewhat different character. The use of the final -*e* enables the writer to employ a large number of feminine rimes; and it will be interesting to see in what proportion they occur. This can only be ascertained by help of a grammatically printed text, such as we find in the version of The Hous of Fame, as given both in S. and G., which differ very little. In the First book of The Hous of Fame (the fittest to choose, on account of its metre), there are about 125 feminine or double rimes out of 254 (508 lines); or roughly speaking, a little less than half of them. In the course of the first 508 lines of The Romaunt, there are about 117 [1] double rimes, or within 8 of the same proportion; a result which is sufficiently satisfactory.

If, to take another point, we examine the treatment in rime of the open and close *ō*, and of the open and close *ē*, in Fragment A, we find that it is fairly consistent with Chaucer's usage. Thus the long open *o* appears in such rimes as *also, so,* 33 ; *tho, ago,* 49 ; *clothe, bothe,* 95 ; *anon, gon* (= *anòòn, gòòn*), 99, 135 ; *forgo, two,* 201 ; *loth, cloth,* 233 ; *also, wo,* 311 ; *wo, two,* 337 ; *noon, gon,* 357 ; *everichoon, aloon,* 449 ; *oon, noon,* 491 ; *noon, goon,* 513 ; &c. The only example which I have observed as being abnormal is the riming of *upòn* (with short open *o*) with *òòn,* 563, and with *stòòn,* 1086. But this has its parallel in the riming of *upòn* with *gòòn* ; C. T., Group G, 562.

Examples of long close *o* appear in *sone, done,* 23 ; *domes, gromes,* 199 ; *wood, good,* 203, 263 ; *good, blood,* 267 ; *good, wood,* 275 ; *to, do,* 757 ; *dome, brome,* 911 ; *swote, rote,* 1025 ; *do, to,* 1221 ; *took, forsook,* 1537 ; *undo, to,* 1633 ; *swote, rote,* 1661. All with *o* or *oo* from an older *ō*.

Examples of long open *e* (from A.S. *ǣ* or *ēa*) appear

---

[1] For this purpose, it is safer to consult S., as the copy in G. follows the MS., and is so ungrammatical as to require much correction.

in *èèk, lèèk,* 211; *dèèd* (dead), *brèèd,* 215; *sprède, rède,*
1679.

Examples of the same (lengthened from A.S. *e*) appear
in *fèle, stèle,* 189; cf. *brède* (A.S. *ǣ*), *stède* (A.S. *e*), 825;
*answère, hère,* 1259.

Examples of close long *e* (from A.S. *ē* or *ēo*) are common;
as in *seen, been,* 3; *be, nycetee,* 11; *me, be,* 15; &c. Note
*tene, sene,* 157; *grene, wene,* 493, 731; *swete, unmete,* 751;
*semen, demen,* 1011; *bene, quene,* 1265; *shete, mete,* 1341.

**65.** Of course the most interesting examples are those
which present some difficulty, as when we find the *third*
variety of *ē* involved, as explained in § 45. This variety,
arising from A.S. *ie,* Mercian *ē,* or from A.S. *ǣ* as due to
gradation, is well exemplified in Fragment A; and I mark
these vowels, as before, with the symbol *ê.*

Accordingly, the following rime with close *ē*; *grene, sêne,*
57; *swete, sête,* 713; *wêre, y-fere,* 785; *dere, nêre,* 1453; *grene,
shêne,* 1511; *grene, sêne,* 1581. Cf. C. T., A 1509, 2297.

The following rime with open *ē*; *nêde, brède,* 1123, 1365;
*lède, drêde,* 1321; *wêre, thère,* or *thêre,* 455, 515, 663, 703,
815, 1297, 1303, 1315, 1409, 1599, 1645, 1675; *rède, mêde,*
1433. Note also *drêde, mêde,* 131; *hère* (G. *Haar*), *thère,*
327; *dêde, hêde,* 417; *wêre, bêre,* 1372; *nêde, drêde,* 1441;
*sêd, rêd,* 1617. Cf. C. T., F 455, B 657.

We further find the suffix *-hede* riming (in contradiction
to etymology) with the close *ē,* as in *yonghede, fede,* 351; but
also with an open *ē,* as in *childhede, lède,* 399; *lède, semeli-
hede,* 1129. And this is one of Chaucer's peculiarities; cf.
*wommanhede, forbede* (from A.S. *forbēodan*), C. T., E 1075;
and, on the other hand, *hèèd* (head), *maydenheed,* D 887.

But the most startling thing is the double use of 'eke.'
In one passage, Fragment A has *èèk,* monosyllabic and
with open *ē,* riming with *lèèk,* 211; but elsewhere it has
*êke,* dissyllabic and with neutral *ē,* riming with *seke,* 533, 561,
*unmeke,* 589, and *chêke,* 1023.

And this, once more, is one of Chaucer's peculiarities; for *èèk* rimes with *lèèk*, C. T., D 571; and *êke* rimes with *seke*, B 60, *meke*, B 716, and *chêke*, D 792! Cf. p. 52.

**66.** In fact, the more closely we examine Fragment A, the more obvious its genuineness becomes; but I shall just add two more considerations.

The first is curious, viz. that (as shown in Chaucer's Works, vi. p. xxiii) Chaucer sometimes employs the Kentish *e* instead of the Midland short *i*. An example occurs in one of his earliest works, viz. in The Book of the Duchesse, 438, where *ken* is used in place of *kin*, to secure a rime with *ten*. And Fragment A has the same peculiarity; we find *knet* in place of *knit*, 1397, in order to rime with *set*[1].

The second consideration is of much importance, as it furnishes us with express *external* testimony, and was only discovered by me when editing the Chaucerian Pieces in 1897 (pref. p. xliv). Lydgate, in the course of his Complaint of the Black Knight, supposed to have been written in 1402, actually quotes from Fragment A expressly, and must have had it before him! For it so happens that he quotes just the very words which are NOT in the French original.

The French has (l. 1399):—

'Entor les ruisseaus et les rives
Des fontaines cleres et vives
Poignoit l'erbe freschete et drue.'

Fragment A translates it thus (l. 1417):—

'About *the brinkes* of thise welles
And by the stremes over-al elles
*Sprang up the gras*, as thikke y-set
And *softe as any veluët*.'

[1] Chaucer also uses repetitions, as in *seke, seke*, C. T., A 17. So also Fragment A has *leef, leef*, 847; cf. *laas, solas*, 843; *archaungel, aungel*, 915. Further, Fragment A never rimes *-ighte* with *-yte*, nor *-ight* with *-yt*.

This Lydgate reproduces thus (Blk. Knt. 78):—

'The gravel gold, the water pure as glas,
The bankes rounde, the welle *envyroning*,
And *softe as veluët, the* yonge *gras*
That *therupon* lustíly cam *springing*.'

We thus find Lydgate, who expressly took Chaucer as his
model, quoting from Fragment A soon after his master's
death.

It is worth while to add a few more resemblances which
Lydgate *might* have obtained from the original; for it is
just as likely that he took them from Fragment A.   Compare—

'Ful cleer was than the morow-tyde,
And ful *attempre*, out of drede.
Tho gan I walke through the mede, . . .
The *river-syde costeying*.
And whan I had a whyle goon,
I saw *a garden* right anoon,
Ful long and brood, . . and *walled wel* . . .
Tho gan I go a ful gret pas
Envyroning even *in compas*
The closing of the square wal
Til that I fond *a wiket smal*.'

Romaunt, 130, 525.

'The eyre *attempre*, and the smothe winde...
And *by a river* forth *I gan costey*
Of water clere as berel or cristal
Til at the laste I found a litel wey
Toward *a park, enclosed with a wal*
*In compas round*, and by *a gate smal*,' &c.

Blk. Knt. 57 ; 36–40.

Several other parallelisms are pointed out in the Notes
to Chaucerian Poems, pp. 504–506.   Thus Lydgate mentions Narcissus (87); cf. Romaunt, 1468.   He uses the

expression *floures inde* (127); cf. R. 67. And he imitates
a convenient pair of rimes in the following instance :—

> 'And forth *his heed* and nekke out-straughte
> *To drinken* of *that welle a draughte*'; R. 1515.
> 'And with *myn heed* unto *the welle* I raughte,
> And of the water *drank I a* good *draughte*';
> Blk. Knt. 111.

L. 1516 of The Romaunt, just quoted, is the *latest* line
in which any verbal imitation by Lydgate occurs. He
shows no knowledge of Fragment B.

**67.** The above important fact, that Lydgate was
obviously acquainted with Fragment A, and was glad to
adopt phrases from it, seems to me to clench all the preceding arguments. In fact, its genuineness is no longer
seriously questioned ; and it is a pleasure to see it now
quoted as CHAUCER's by both the editors of the New
English Dictionary, as, e.g., s. vv. *Girdlestead* and *Habit*,
verb. But it seemed to me worth while to give a fairly
complete proof of this interesting result [1].

**68.** The date assigned to Fragment A in the New Eng.
Dict. is about 1366. This must be very near the truth,
since Chaucer was already familiar with *Le Roman* when
writing The Book of the Duchesse in 1369 ; and we may
call to mind that, in 1366, Chaucer was already about twenty-
six years of age or a little more. Several parallel passages
from his other works may be compared ; see Works, vol. i.
pp. 470–2, 474–5, 477–8. I here quote the first that
occurs :—

> 'But undoth us th'avisioun
> That whylom mette king Scipioun'; R.R., 9, 10.
> 'He that wroot al th'avisioun
> That he mette, king Scipioun'; Bk. Duch. 285–6.

[1] See Note at p. 149.

# CHAPTER VII

THE ROMAUNT OF THE ROSE : FRAGMENT B

**69.** IT will be seen, from the above chapter, how very strong is the case in favour of Fragment A, and how it satisfies every test that can fairly be applied. The very completeness of this case is fatal to the pretensions of Fragment B, because the latter fails to satisfy nearly every test that exists. Try it how we will, it breaks down miserably, completely, fatally.

The latest word said in its defence is but a poor one, and is founded on much misconception. It is said that the class of argument employed to demonstrate its spuriousness 'rests on extremely minute points of linguistics, phonetics, and other "sciences of the border," as we may perhaps call them, [and] seems to demand an equal specialism from those who would attempt to meet it.' This statement is doubly misleading, for it so happens that the separation of Fragment B from Fragment A was, originally, a *literary* discovery, entirely independent of linguistics ; and secondly, the amount of ' specialism ' demanded is merely such an acquaintance with Sweet's Anglo-Saxon Primer as many students (including women) frequently acquire in a few months ; or indeed, the arguments can be followed by any one, with even moderate ability, who can make shift to follow to some extent the arguments contained in the preceding chapters of the present volume. All turns upon the ability to comprehend

the grammatical usages of the Ormulum, which are founded
upon those exemplified in the Anglo-Saxon Primer. Indeed, any one who has so much knowledge of modern
German as to comprehend that *ich dacht* and *ich habe
gedachte* are both incorrect, and who knows what they
ought to be, will not experience much difficulty. Just
a moderate amount of common sense, docility, and patience
is needed; and that is all. In every case of doubt, re-
course can be had to the Canterbury Tales, which contains
an almost inexhaustible fund of information as to Chaucer's
methods. Let it be granted that Chaucer wrote those
Tales; and it follows, almost as a matter of course, that
he wrote Fragment A of The Romaunt, and did *not* write
Fragment B. Of course there was a time, a few years ago,
when these results were disputed; but there comes a time
when arguments which can so easily be verified by any
serious student can no longer be ignored or creditably
dismissed.

70. I have said that the original discovery as to Fragment B was of a literary character. All that has to be done
is to recapitulate the story.

A critical edition of the Glasgow MS. was undertaken
for the Chaucer Society by Dr. Max Kaluza, of Königs-
berg, which ultimately appeared in 1891. The editor was
at the pains to give a French text of *Le Roman* at the same
time, choosing a MS. which seemed to agree better than
most with the English version. In comparing the English
with the original French line by line, and word by word,
he discovered—what any one else would have discovered if
he had taken equal care and pains—that soon after l. 1700,
the literary character and style of the English version are
very materially altered. The same French words receive
new translations, whilst the version is much more loose
and prolix. In Fragment A, the translation runs nearly
line for line; or to be exact, its 1705 lines answer to 1678

lines of French, in the proportion of 101·6 to 100. But
in Fragment B, the translator employs, on an average,
11 lines and three-quarters for every 10 of the original;
or to be exact, its 4105 lines answer to 3491 of the original,
in the proportion of 117·5 to 100. The difference is
obvious and startling; and the fact is less linguistic than
literary. No quibbling can explain it away. The change
of style is also clearly marked, when once attention has
been drawn to it. There is a certain lightness of touch,
a pleasing playfulness about Fragment A, which—unless
I am mistaken—is less conspicuous in Fragment B; and
I can only record my own experience that, as the poem
progresses, it becomes drearier; but this is only a personal impression, which may contradict the experience of
others, and is of no value in itself. Moreover, it is very
difficult to give an instance of what I mean; but I will
just give *one* example. In *Le Roman*, where we find 'Car
Cupido, li fils Venus,' Chaucer gives us (l. 1616) the
version 'For Venus sone, *daun* Cupido,' where the introduction of *daun* is a touch of his own[1]. I am far from
saying that Fragment B is not well done, but I believe it
will be found, upon analysis, that the manner and style of
it are not those of Chaucer. But this is too difficult
a question to be pursued here.

At any rate, the difference in the mode of translation
was so marked that Dr. Kaluza was able to see the distinction clearly. In particular, he noticed that whereas, in
lines 1675, 1683, 1685, and 1691, the F. *bouton* or *boutons*
was translated by *knoppes*, and in l. 1702 by *knoppe*, the
English word became *botoun* in ll. 1721, 1761, 1770, 1786,
&c. The break is therefore between l. 1702 and 1721;
but it is easy to come nearer than this. For at l. 1705

[1] Cf. the example (cited in § 66) in l. 1420—'And softe as any
veluët,' added by the translator. As for 'daun Cupido,' he reappears
in The Hous of Fame, 137.

comes the first false rime—*aboute* as a rime to *swote*; and in l. 1707 comes the first trace of non-Chaucerian dialect, in the use of *thens yit* for *thennes*. Hence Dr. Kaluza drew the line of demarcation between l. 1704 and 1705. But I at once pointed out to him that the obvious break is rather at l. 1705, to which he at once agreed. For at the end of l. 1705 we have a complete dislocation in the sense. The sentence begins with—'That it dide al the place aboute'—and then comes to a sudden end, without any conclusion[1]. L. 1706 starts a new clause, and at the same time exhibits a non-Chaucerian rime.

**71.** We have seen, *a priori*, from purely literary considerations, that Fragment B is separated from A by its greater diffuseness and by its change of style; and it is difficult to understand why these considerations should not, in themselves, suffice to settle the question. Nor is this all; for before we come to apply grammatical tests, a new and startling difficulty arises in the fact that we have to deal with *a change of dialect!* This incontrovertible fact ought, once again, to give us pause; and we have a right to enquire how it is to be explained away.

The truth is, that the English employed in Fragment B is artificial and unnatural, like that of The Kingis Quair and Lancelot of the Laik. The author's natural dialect was some form of Northumbrian, but he had so thoroughly steeped himself in the study of Southern poetry, and, of course, in that of Chaucer in particular, that he had picked up most of the peculiarities of Southern grammar, and

---

[1] Even if Chaucer translated the *whole* of the Romaunt (which, when we regard its preposterous length, exceeding that of the Canterbury Tales, really seems a little doubtful), it is conceivable that he only revised it, for preservation, as far as l. 1705. The stopping in the middle of a sentence is so very characteristic; observe the condition of the Squieres Tale, the Hous of Fame, the Legend, and the Astrolabe.

makes a parade of his use of the final -*e* in many places; but this he does so capriciously and artificially that he often forgets all about it, especially in the case of rimes, where he ought to have been most careful. However, there is no reason for supposing that he ever intended or expected his work to be mistaken for Chaucer's. He did not know that printing would one day be invented, that his work would be revived by Thynne in all the glory of print, and that there would be a future race of critics who could not tell Northern dialect from Southern.

The simple supposition that Fragment B was written by a Northerner, who imitated Chaucer's diction and grammar rather carefully, but reverted to what was habitual to him whenever he forgot what Chaucer's system of rimes demanded, will explain all and every of the numerous anomalies with which this specimen of English abounds.

It explains, for example, the very first anomalous rime that presents itself, viz. the rime of *aboute* with *swote*. It is clear that the author came upon Fragment A just as it is now, i. e. in an imperfect condition, ending with the word *aboute*. He either did not perceive that the sense was incomplete, or he hardly knew how to complete it. At any rate, he started a new sentence, beginning with an equivalent for the French line—'Quand ge le senti si flairier,' adopting 'the savour swote' from 'The savour of the roses swote' in l. 1661. For him, the word *aboute* would be sounded as mod. E. *aboot*, and the word *swōte* would be sounded very nearly as mod. E. *swoot*, instead of keeping the A.S. long close *o*, as in the Southern English of that date[1]. That is, he considered the rime sufficiently good, and was quite contented. It will soon

---

[1] The student should refer constantly, throughout Fragment B, to Barbour's Bruce and Blind Harry's Wallace. The *ō* and *ū* came out nearly alike in Northern. See Dr. F. J. Curtis, on the Rimes in Clariodus, Halle, 1894 ; § 530 (g). Barbour has *touk* for *took*, ii. 553.

appear that, for him, the final -*e* was an artificial embellish-ment.

**72.** When once we hold this clue to Fragment B, and realise that we are dealing with a Northern writer, who in many instances successfully imitates Chaucer's grammar by dint of memory, but sometimes forgets his lesson, there is no more difficulty. Perhaps it will be easiest to con-sider, first of all, the cases in which the peculiarities of his Northern dialect are obvious and unconcealed.

(*a*) Very striking is his use of the Northern pres. par-ticiple in -*and*, as seen in Barbour's Bruce. We find the following examples :—

> ' Poyntis and sleves be wel *sittand*,
> Right and streighte upon the *hand*'; 2263.
> ' They shal hir telle how they thee fand
> Curteis and wys, and wel *doand*'; 2707.

Here the forms *sittand* and *doand* are not due to the scribe, but to the author; for they cannot be altered to *sitting* and *doing* without wholly destroying the rimes. Consequently, we can see that the forms *lepand* for *leping* in l. 1928, *sparand* for *sparing* in l. 5363, and *criand* for *crying* in l. 3138, are also due to the author. Indeed, it is easy to see that the scribe was not himself a Northerner, for he has much mitigated the Northern aspect of the poem. This is why the suffix of the pres. participle commonly appears as -*ing*. But of course he was powerless to alter the forms *sittand* and *doand* when they occurred in rimes. For the same reason, he let the form *fand* remain in l. 2707. The Midland form was *fond*; see twenty-four examples of it in the Glossarial Index to Chaucer's Works.

(*b*) In lines 1853–4, we find the rimes *thore* and *more*, due to the scribe; read *thar* (there) and *mar* (more), and we get a perfect Northern rime. Replace them by the

Chaucerian forms *there* and *more*[1], and we get no rime at all.

At l. 2215, we find a similar phenomenon : the rime *ar*, *mar* is correct, but it is unluckily only possible in Northern. Replace these words by the Chaucerian forms *aren* and *more*, and again we get no rime at all.

At l. 2397, the riming words are *stat* and *hat*; where *hat* is Northern for 'hot.' Replace them by the Chaucerian forms *stat* and *hoot*; and again we get no rime at all.

At l. 4199, we find the words *made* and *brade*, which only rime in Northern. The Chaucerian forms *maad* or *mad* and *bròdë* will not rime at all.

At l. 4421, we find *wil, thertil*; but *thertil* belongs to the Northern dialect. Chaucer's word is *therto*.

No less than six times do we find *slo* (to slay) riming with *go*; 1953, 3149, 3523, 4591, 4991, 5643 ; and once it rimes with *a-two*, 5521. It will rime as it stands, or in Northern, i. e. in the forms *sla, ga, a-twa*. But Chaucer's form, unluckily, happens to be *slee*. Cf. pp. 104–5.

At l. 5399, we find the Northern rime *wat, estat*. Chaucer's forms are *woot* or *wot, estat* ; which do not rime.

At l. 5457, we find the Northern rime *bare, ware* (better as *bar, war*). Chaucer's forms are *bare, were* ; giving no rime at all at that period, because the *a* in *bare* was still pronounced like the *a* in *bar*.

So again *spare, ware* (better *spar, war*), at l. 5637. Chaucer's forms *spare, were* give no rime at all.

So again *ware, forfare* (better *war, forfar*) at l. 5777. Chaucer's forms *were, forfare*, give no rime at all.

To these facts no reply is possible ; so it is pleaded that it requires 'specialism' to understand them. As if nothing can be true unless it is obvious to every untaught child.

(*c*) But more, even much more, remains. The amusing

---

[1] For Chaucerian forms, see the Glossarial Index to the Works.

point is to observe how the author forgets his final -*e* at
the end of the line, precisely where it is of most importance, as it helps to form the richer or feminine rime.   It is
much as if an imitator of Dante were to employ *cricch* to
rime with *ricchi*, being quite unconscious of any difference [1].

To recount such errors takes up almost more space than
they are worth.   To save trouble, I give *only* the Chaucerian forms and the references.   The reader who has no
'special' knowledge can verify such forms by help of the
Glossary.   It will be seen that in all the following instances
the true Chaucerian rime has been destroyed.

Observe *grew, hew-e,* 1789; *hit, flit-te,* 1811; *ther-e,*
*to-shar,* 1857; *bow-e, prow,* 1939; *feet, let-e,* 1981; *may,*
*obey-e,* 1995; *been, wen-e,* 2045; *ay, pley-e,* 2321; *depart-e,*
*part,* 2367; *son-e, doon,* 2377; *peyn-e, again,* 2411; *wen-e,*
*been,* 2415; *may, convey-e,* 2427; *wit-e, it,* 2519; *dight-e,*
*delyt,* 2555; *set, get-e,* 2615; *spring-e, thing,* 2627; *ly-e, by,*
2629; *ly-e, erly,* 2645; *by-e, tenderly,* 2737; *set, et-e,* 2755;
*set, get-e,* 2855; *sey-e, may,* 2867; &c., &c.   Surely it is
needless to go further.   Why are there no such instances
in Fragment A?

(*d*) But there is more yet.   For it is in this Fragment
only that we find mere assonances and very imperfect rimes.

Here are the assonances: *kepe, eke,* 2125; *shape, make,*
2250; *escape, make,* 2753; *take, scape,* 3165; *storm, corn,*
4343; *doun, tourn,* 5469.

And here are rimes which it were a gross libel to
attribute to Chaucer; *aboute, swote,* 1705-6; *desyre, nere,*
1785, 2441; *abrede, forwerede,* 2563; *anney* (Ch. has *annoy*),
*awey,* 2675; *desyre, manere,* 2779; *Ioye, convoye,* (Ch. has
*conveye*), 2915; *lere, desyre,* 4685.

(*e*) Of course the author pays no attention at all to

---

[1] At the end of a line, where the reader can pause, the additional
syllable is always fully uttered.   Dante does not use *cammin* at the
end of a line, but only *cammino.*

Chaucer's distinction between words ending in -*y* and those ending in -*yë*.

So he ignorantly mixes them after this sort : *I, malady-e*, 1849 ; *hastily, company-e*, 1861 ; *generally, vilany-e*, 2179 ; *worthy, curtesy-e*, 2209 ; *foly-e, by*, 2493, 2521 ; *curtesy-e, gladly*, 2985 ; *foly-e, utterly*, 3171 ; *foly-e, hastily*, 3241, 3289 ; *redily, maistry-e*, 3293 ; *flatery-e, uttirly*, 3387 ; *angerly, vilany-e*, 3511 ; *espy-e, sikirly*, 3815 ; *folily, Ielosy-e*, 3819 ; *Ielosy-e, I*, 3909, 4145 ; *certeynly, Ielosy-e*, 4047 ; *sikirly, foly-e*, 4469 ; *bittirly, foly-e*, 4533 ; *I, curtesy-e*, 4565 ; &c., &c. If Chaucer wrote Fragment B, why do no such rimes appear in Fragment A? It is not as if the rule were at all intricate ; a large number of such examples are covered by remarking that Chaucer does not rime adverbs in -*ly* with French feminine substantives in -*yë*, such as *foly-ë*. Quite a small effort of attention will enable the mind to grasp the principle of it.

(*f*) By way of change, let us note a pure question of literary style. In l. 1275, Chaucer translates the French *sans faille* by *withouten fayle* ; but he twice introduces the phrase *withouten wene*, 574, 732, and once the phrase *withouten drede*, 1442, as mere tags, to complete lines. In the course of 1705 lines, this is not very noticeable and may be pardoned. But I think it shows bad taste on the part of the author of Fragment B to introduce similar tags with such persistent frequency. Thus he gives us *withouten drede* thrice, 2199, 2251, 4503; *withoute doute* twice, 2967, 3615; *withouten fable*, 4687 ; *withoute gesse*, 2819; *withouten lees* twice, 3904, 5728; *without lesing*, 4508 ; *withouten lette*, 3756 ; *withoute more* thrice, 1895, 3195, 3763 ; *withoute wene* at least nine times, 2046, 2415, 2595, 2668, 2683, 3231, 3641, 3748, 4596; and *withouten were* at least seven times, 1776, 2568, 2740, 3351, 3452, 5485, 5657. I found no argument upon this, but I do not find these thirty tags attractive.

73. It is hardly worth while to pursue the subject in this direction. Other numerous objections to the genuineness of Fragment B can easily be adduced when those already given have been satisfactorily met. It remains to consider the probable date of this poem. The chief fact is that the Glasgow MS., very neatly written, cannot well be later than 1440. The only other consideration that helps us is to remember that, whilst an imitator would hardly copy Chaucer's grammatical forms until after that poet's death, when his reputation was at its height, we should nevertheless expect the imitation to be not very late[1]. A very likely date would be about 1420; though this, it will be understood, is only a guess.

I remember once discussing the question with Professor Seeley, who, half in jest and half in earnest, suggested that, if Fragment B was not written by Chaucer, he would be glad to attribute it to king James I. It is singular that there is no vital objection to this rather bold suggestion; indeed, there are many points in its favour. For the king being born in 1394, and captured by the English in 1406[2], remained in captivity till 1424, and had ample opportunity of studying Chaucer's writings. This is too large a question to be considered here; and unfortunately, the King's Quair is too short a poem to furnish us with much linguistic information. I will merely say that it affords several rimes involving Northern forms, such as *begouth*, st. 16; *fand*, st. 79; *hing* (they hang), st. 89; *Iunyt* (joined), st. 133; and rimes such as *ageyn* riming with *to pleyn*, st. 40, which in

---

[1] The partial use of the final -*e*, which was fast disappearing soon after 1400, shows that neither the King's Quair nor our Fragment B are likely to be late.

[2] I take these dates from J. T. T. Brown, The Authorship of the Kingis Quair, Glasgow, 1896; p. 21. I do not accept his conclusion, that the Kingis Quair was imitated from the Court of Love. For the Court of Love was the later poem of the two; and both poems contain imitations of Lydgate's Temple of Glass; as proved by Schick.

Chaucer would become *to pleyn-e* (compare § 72 (*c*)); that it has the false rime of *corage* with *charge* and *large*, st. 38 (compare § 72 (*d*)); that it twice has the very rime *Ioye*, *convoye*, stt. 19, 71, to which I have drawn attention above (§ 72 (*d*)); and that it makes no distinction between the suffixes -*y* and -*yë* (see § 72 (*e*) ).

**74.** It is clear that the author of the King's Quair was acquainted with *Le Roman de la Rose*, as he expressly alludes to it in the line—'And has no curage at the rose to pull'—in st. 186; and he adopts from it the word *amorettes*; (st. 47, and note), which occurs in Fragment A, l. 892. And perhaps it is worth noticing a line in the very next stanza, viz. st. 48—'Aboute hir nek, quhite as the fyre amaille' [enamel]. For, although there is nothing remarkable about the phrase 'Aboute hir nekke' in Fragment A, l. 1081, it is a singular coincidence that the last word in the preceding line is the scarce word *ameled* [enamelled]. And next, if we look a little more closely at the same stanza, we shall find that there is a description of a chain hung about the same neck, to which was attached a ruby that shone like a spark of fire. This I take to be Chaucer's carbuncle, mentioned only forty lines farther on, which enabled people to travel a mile or two by night-time, because 'such light sprang out of the stone.' If, again, we look at st. 46, preceding that which contains *amorettis*, we shall find mention of rich attire, emeralds and sapphires, which may very well have been suggested by the same passage, descriptive of the fine clothing worn by Richesse :—

> '*Rubyes* there were, *saphyres*, jagounces,
> And *emeraudes*, more than two ounces';
>                                        R. R. 1117.

The ruby, as already noted, occurs in K. Q. st. 48.

A comparison of K. Q. stt. 46–48 with Fragment A shows

a sufficient general resemblance to be worth considering. With *goldin hair*, cf. R. 1021, 'Hir tresses yelowe'; with *rich atyre*, cf. R. 1071; for emeralds and sapphires, see R. 1117; for chaplets, see R. 563, 845, 908; for *amorettis*, see R. 892; for 'Beautee eneuch to make a world to dote,' see the description of Beauty in R. 1009–1032; the phrase 'aboute hir nekke' occurs fifty lines further on, R. 1081, preceded by the word *ameled*; for the ruby, cf. R. 1117 (just quoted), and for its resplendent light, see R. 1121. With *tissew* in st. 49, cf. R. 1104. It does not amount to much, but it seems enough.

**75.** A second passage, stt. 152–7, does not contain much from The Romaunt, but there is something[1]. The poet travels 'endlang a river,' which puts us on the scent; cf. 'The river-syde costeying,' R. R. 134. We can now compare the following passages :—

> 'Endlang a river, pleasant to behold . . .
> Quhar, through the gravel, bricht as ony gold,
> The cristal water ran so clere and cold.'
>
>                                        K. Q. 152.

> 'Toward a river I gan me dresse,
> That I herde renne faste by;
> For fairer playing non saugh I
> Then playen me by that riveer . . .
> Cleer was the water, and as cold,' &c.
>
>                                        R. R. 110.

The bright gravel is not far off, viz. in l. 127 :—

> 'With gravel, ful of stones shene.'

In stt. 154–7 we have a mention of fruit-trees, followed by the remarkable account of all sorts of animals. The Romaunt contains plenty of fruit-trees in ll. 1359–1400 (we shall have them again below); and though the list

---

[1] This section is reprinted from my letter to The Athenæum (no. 3741) upon this subject, which appeared on July 8, 1899.

of fruit-trees is not followed by an account of a menagerie,
we find the hint of one in the succeeding lines, ll. 1401–
1408 ; and we actually there encounter 'the litil squerel,
ful of businesse,' and 'the rial hart, the coning, and the ro.'
For what says The Romaunt?—

> ' Ther mighte men does and roes y-see,
> And of squirels ful greet plentee,
> From bough to bough alwey leping;
> Conies ther were also pleying.'

The consideration of a third passage, K. Q. stt. 31–3, will
confirm the preceding conclusions, and will bring us at last
face to face with Chaucer's own words :—

> ' Now was ther maid fast by the touris wal
> A gardin fair, and in the corneris set
> An herber grene, with wandis long and smal
> Railit about; and so with treis set
> Was al the place, and hawthorn-hegis knet,
> That lyf was non, walking ther forby,
> That might within scars ony wight aspy.
>
> So thik the bewis and the levis grene
> Beshadit al the aleyes that ther wer . . .
>
> And on the smalë grenë twistis sat
> The litil swetë nightingale, and song . . .'

This takes us back, as I said it would, to the list of
fruit-trees, especially ll. 1387–1400. And it is worth while
to notice that Chaucer himself was the first person to
reproduce the original passage, in his Book of the Duchesse
416–442, where he tells us that he saw green groves, so
thick with trees and leaves that there was shadow everywhere below ; and then he immediately introduces (in the
proper place) the hart and hind, does, roes, and squirrels,
and more beasts than Argus could count.

For the 'gardin fair' and 'the wal' and 'the nightingale,'

see R. R. 136 and 644, 138 and 78.   The rest of the passage is more significant.

The original passage in R. R. 1391–1400 is as follows : —

> 'These trees were set, that I devyse,
> Oon from another, in assyse,
> Five fadome or sixe, I trowe so,
> But they were hye and grete also :
> And for to kepe out wel the sonne,
> The croppes were so thikke y-ronne,
> And every braunch in other knet,
> And ful of grene leves set,
> That sonne mighte noon descende,
> Lest [it] the tendre grasses shende.'

And here it is at last that we come upon the very Chaucer.   For I have shown (Works, vol. vi. p. xxiii) that our great poet, with all his nicety and care in the selection of rhymes, frequently adopts Kentish forms, using *ken* for *kin* (Bk. Duch., 438), *fulfelle* for *fulfille* (Troil. iii. 510), *kesse* for *kisse* (C. T., E 1057), *knette* for *knitte* (Mars, 183, Parl. Foules, 438), and *knet* for *knit*, as in the present passage.   But what business, we may well ask in amazement, had a Scotchman with *a Kentish form*?   He knew perfectly well that the form natural to him was *knit*, for he uses it in K. Q. st. 194, where he rimes it with *wit* and *it*.   The conclusion is obvious : he saw that Chaucer used *knet* as a convenient rhyme with *set*, so he knew that he had authority for doing the same.   In other words, he was not only familiar with *Le Roman de la Rose*, but he was acquainted with, and practically quotes, the very words of Chaucer's own translation.

**76.** From all this we see that the author of the Kingis Quair (whether he was James I or not) was acquainted with Chaucer's version of *Le Roman*, and was capable

(whether he did so or not) of translating it into a mixed
jargon of Northern and Chaucerian English. Perhaps the
reader will now not be surprised to hear that the author
of Fragment B was likewise rather proud of knowing the
form *knet*, as he uses it three times; ll. 2092, 4700, 4811.
He even rimes it with the Kentish form *shet* (2092); a result
which ceases to astonish us when we observe that *shet* occurs
twice in Fragment A, ll. 529, 1082, and at least twenty-five
times in Chaucer. It is odd that l. 1082 is the one that
follows 'Aboute hir nekke.'

We may safely conclude that Fragment B was not
written by Chaucer, but by a Northern imitator; whilst
there is, at the same time, no reason whatever against
ascribing it to King James I. Indeed, there is much to
be said in favour of that supposition [1].

[1] A further argument is that the fine line in Rom. Rose, 5004—'That
Deth stant armed at hir gate'—is not in the original, but was almost
certainly borrowed from Gower's story of 'The Trump of Death,'
C. A., i. 116, 18 ; and Gower's poem was well known to the author of
the King's Quair (st. 197). We may further compare K. Q. st. 53
with 'I pleye with her litel hound' in Gower, C. A. ii. 41; st. 55 with
C. A. ii. 318 ; st. 97, l. 3 with C. A. i. 307; st. 134, ll. 6, 7 with C. A.
i. 76; and st. 140 with C. A. i. 177.

# CHAPTER VIII

## THE ROMAUNT OF THE ROSE: FRAGMENT C

**77.** THAT Fragment C has nothing to do with B is easily seen; for the traces of Northumbrian dialect at once disappear, and we return to a dialect which does not materially differ from that of Fragment A. Moreover, the diffuse treatment seen in B disappears at the same time, and the translation is given, as in A, almost line for line. To be exact, the 1888 lines in C correspond to 1849 lines of the original *Roman*; i.e. in the proportion of 102·1 to 100. The proportion in A is as 101·6 to 100; so that C is a little more diffuse than A, but only to the extent of one half per cent. Lastly, the character called *Bialacoil* throughout Fragment B is called *Fair-welcoming* in C. On many accounts, C is far nearer than B to Chaucer, and has a better chance of being genuine. Nevertheless, I am reluctantly compelled to say that I fear it is not his, for I have found yet more to add to such arguments as I have given already and now repeat here, nearly as in Chaucer's Works, vol. i. p. 6.

**78.** In the first place, C does not, like A, satisfy the test which separates words ending in -*y* from those ending in -*y-ë*. In the course of its 1888 lines, there are six failures of this sort.

The examples are : *covertly, Ipocrisy(e)*, 6111 ; *company(e)*,

*outerly*, 6301 ; *loteby, company'e*), 6339 ; *why, tregetry(e*),
6373 ; *company'e*), *I*, 6875 ; *mekely, trechery(e*), 7319.

Other unsatisfactory rimes are these : *hors* (horse), *wors*
(worse), 5919, whereas Chaucer rimes *wors* with *curs* (Cant.
Tales, A 4349) and with *pervers* (Bk. Duch. 813) ; *fare,*
*are*, 6045, though *are* never ends a line in Chaucer, as
he there uses *been* in place of it ; *atte last, agast,* 6105,
whereas Chaucer only has *atte last-e*, where *last-e* is dissyllabic ; *pati-ence, venge-aunce*, 6429, a very bad rime,
resembling nothing in Chaucer ; and *force, croce*, 6469,
which is hardly a rime at all.

Further, we find *preched* riming with *teched*, 6679, whereas
Chaucer uses the form *taughte*, as in C. T., prol. 497.
Another unsatisfactory feature is the use of the form *Ab-
stinaunce* in l. 7483 (7481 in G.), to rime with *penaunce*, whilst
only twenty-two lines further on it becomes *Abstinence*, to
rime with *sentence* ; however, the original French text has
a similar variation.   See further in § 79.

**79.** I will here also mention one more peculiarity to
be found in Fragment C.   In the Cant. Tales, B 480 (and
elsewhere), Chaucer employs such rimes as *clerkes, derk is,*
and the like ; but not very often.   But the author of
Fragment C was fond of this peculiarity, and has eight
instances in the course of his 1888 lines.   Such are :
*requestis, honèst is,* 6039 ; *places, place is,* 6119 ; *nede is,*
*dedis,* 6659 ; *apert is, certis,* 6799 ; *chaïéris, dere is,* 6915 ;
*enquestes, honèst is,* 6977 ; *prophetis, prophéte is,* 7093 ;
*ypocrítis, spite is,* 7253 (7251 in G.).   The proportion of such
rimes in Chaucer is much smaller, viz. five in the 2158 lines
of The Hous of Fame, which is in the same metre as the
Romaunt, and nineteen in the Canterbury Tales.   The per-
centages are :—in Fragment B, ·423 ; in the Hous of Fame,
·231 ; and in the Cant. Tales, ·109.

The above difficulties, as I have just said, have already
been pointed out by me in a former work.   But I now

find that several serious false rimes remain to be noticed. I take them in the order of their occurrence.

At l. 6665, we find *honden*, hands, to rime with *undirstonden*; but Chaucer has *hondes* or *handes*.

At l. 6717, we have the rime *science, ignorence*; but *ignorence*, in Chaucer, appears as *ignoraunce*.

At l. 7091, we have the rime of *Christendōme* with *sŏmme*, some. Chaucer never rimes long close *ō* with the short *ŏ* which does duty for A.S. *u*. It would be a gross libel to charge him with it.

At l. 7137, we find the rime *del* (deal) riming with *wil* (they will); French text, 'garderont.' There is no way, that I know, of justifying such an atrocity.

At l. 7198 (7196 in G.), the gerund *fighte* is cut down to *fight*, to rime with the sb. *might*.

Here are five insuperable difficulties, to add to those that have been mentioned already.

In Englische Studien, xi. 163, Dr. Lindner wrote an article in which he came to the conclusion that Chaucer certainly never wrote Fragment C.

**80.** It seems to me possible to account for Fragment C very easily, without any reference to Chaucer. There is a very good reason why it should be separated from Fragment B by more than 5000 lines of the French *Roman*. It is quite complete in itself, having no relation to the preceding Fragments. It is clear, upon consideration, that its author never dreamt of translating the whole poem, but wished to give what may fairly be called the episode or story of False Semblant or Hypocrisy. It was easy to see where this story ended, for there is a clear break at the very point where he stops. But it was difficult to know where to begin; and I am prepared to maintain that he began at the only possible place. The beginning is somewhat abrupt; but this was the fault of Jean de Meun, who introduces, just at this point, some wholly irrelevant personal details about himself and Guillaume de Lorris, concluding with the lines :—

> 'Ainsinc Amors à eus parole,
> Qui bien reçurent sa parole';—

i. e. 'Thus Love harangues them, and they received his story graciously'; which was very generous of them. Then he goes on by saying :—

> 'Quant il ot sa reison fenie,
> Conseilla soi la baronnie':—

that is to say (as our author puts it) :—

> 'Whan Love had told hem his entente
> The baronage to councel wente.'

All that is wanted to introduce the story are a few words such as these : 'At last Love pities the lover, and descends to help him; and with the assistance of Bounty, Honour, and other barons of Love's court, proceeds to lay siege to the castle in which Jealousy has imprisoned Fair-Reception.' Even without this preliminary introduction, the reader soon finds his way. In a word, the translator of Fragment C selected a fair specimen of Jean de Meun at his best, and has given us his account of Hypocrisy with some spirit, in as complete a form as was practicable. And this is the best reason for supposing that this translator had nothing to do either with Chaucer or his Northern continuator.

All that we can say is that he was one who was attracted rather by religious satire than by romance, one who sympathised, probably, with the author of The Plowman's Tale. The grammatical forms are fairly correct and not late; and this Fragment may have been written as early as 1390. The author was not in the position of a continuator, but assumed an independent attitude of his own.

# CHAPTER IX

**81.** THE most important book, with regard to the Chaucerian canon, is of course Thynne's first edition of Chaucer
in 1532, as this was the first volume in which his Works
were presented in a collected form.

Thynne's second edition, in 1542, was a mere reprint,
introducing more misprints; the only additional piece
being The Plowman's Tale, which was inserted at *the end*
of the Canterbury Tales as a sort of supplement; for the
three minor pieces, introduced at the end of the Table of
Contents, viz. Eight goodly questions, To the Knights of
the Garter, and Sayings, appear in the *first* edition also, in
the same strange position.

About 1550 appeared an undated edition, a mere reprint
of the second edition and with further misprints, in which
The Plowman's Tale was inserted *before* The Parson's Tale,
as if it were really one of the set. Taking advantage of
the fact that this edition is undated, it is frequently pretended that the real date is about 1537, as an excuse for
raising the price; and this is the origin of the fabulous
edition of 'about 1537,' which will long continue to appear
in sale-catalogues. This edition likewise has the three
minor pieces above mentioned, in the same strange position.

In 1561 appeared Stowe's edition, part of which is
a mere reprint of the third undated edition, with yet more

misprints; but it added a considerable number of new pieces, of which the longest are The Court of Love and Lydgate's Siege of Thebes.

In 1598 appeared Speght's first edition, which added Chaucer's Dream and The Flower and the Leaf.

In 1602 appeared Speght's second edition, which added Jack Upland and Chaucer's A B C.

For full details, see Chaucer's Works, vol. i. pp. 31–48; and consult the List at the end of the present volume.

The first four editions are most easily distinguished by observing the spelling of the eighth line of The Plowman's Tale; as thus :—

Ed. 1532. *No* Plowman's Tale.

Ed. 1542. And honge his harneys on a pynne; fol. cxix.

Ed. [1550]. And honged his harnys on a pynne; fol. xciii.

Ed. 1561. And honged his harnis on a pinne; fol. xc.

Observe the progress of error. In ed. 1542, the verb *honge* is strong, but later it is weak. In ed. 1542, *harneys* means 'harness' or 'gear.' But the *e* drops out of *harneys* in the next edition, after which Stowe turns it into *harnis*, the usual word for 'brains.' How the Plowman hanged his brains on a pin, it is difficult to tell.

**82.** Much that has been written on the canon of Chaucer's Works is practically worthless and misleading, owing to the extraordinary way in which Thynne's collection of Middle-English poems has been misunderstood. Just because a considerable number of the poems included in it happened to be by Chaucer, the bookbinders naturally put 'Chaucer's Works' on the back of the volume, and the booksellers called it 'Chaucer's Works' for short. The appearance in it of any given piece affords *no* presumption that such a piece is Chaucer's, unless there is some external evidence in its favour. Yet some critics are pleased to say that the inclusion of a piece in that particular volume is equivalent to 'attributing' it to Chaucer!

At this rate, the following pieces are certainly his, in spite of Thynne's own titles :—

Iohn Gower vnto the worthy and noble kynge Henry the fourthe.

Scogan vnto the lordes and gentylmen of the kynges house.

The truth is, simply, that not a single piece in the whole collection can be taken on trust *as being Chaucer's*. We must really condescend to examine the evidence from other quarters.

We find, for example, that The Testament of Creseide is printed by Thynne in a travesty of a Scottish dialect; and we all know why. It was notoriously written by Robert Henryson.

We find, in The Letter of Cupide, an assertion by the author that he wrote the poem in 1402, when Chaucer had been dead two years. And we know what this means; for the piece is by Hoccleve.

The climax is reached when we learn that Thynne was actually dissuaded by the king from inserting The Pilgrim's Tale, which *he knew* to have been written less than six years previously, viz. in 1536, as it contained an allusion to Perkin Warbeck [1]. If The Pilgrim's Tale had been inserted, it would have been 'attributed to Chaucer'; at least, so some critics tell us. But it is best to look at things for ourselves.

**83.** The result is rather extraordinary. I have shown, in the Introduction to Chaucerian Pieces, that the number of authors represented in Thynne's Collection is more than a dozen, of whom not less than eight are known by name, viz. Usk, Gower, Hoccleve, Scogan, Lydgate, Ros, Henryson, and Clanvowe. And amongst these, Hoccleve is responsible for two pieces, and Lydgate for at

---

[1] F. Thynne, Animadversions on Speght's Chaucer, ed. Furnivall, p. 10. 'Perkyn werbek' is mentioned in The Pilgrim's Tale at l. 447.

least six. And as we thus know, at the very outset, that *at least fourteen* of the pieces are positively *not* Chaucer's, it at once becomes obvious that every piece must be considered on its own merits and without prejudgement. I shall now give the names of the principal pieces which must certainly be excluded from the canon, though they appear in Thynne's two editions. Pieces which were added to the Collection by later editors will be considered afterwards.

**84.** Only three of these pieces were written in Chaucer's lifetime, viz. The Testament of Love, The Plowman's Tale, and The Praise of Peace.

**The Testament of Love**; by Thomas Usk; ab. 1387. (Ch. Pieces, no. I. p. 1.) No MS. is known.

This is a tedious prose treatise in three Books. Thynne was quite justified, from his own point of view, in including this piece, for he happened to have access to it, and it would otherwise have perished. Moreover it clearly belonged to the fourteenth century, and was connected with Chaucer by the fact that it refers to him in Bk. iii. ch. 4.

'Quod Love, "I shal telle thee, this lesson to lerne. Myne owne trewe servaunt, the noble philosophical poete in Englissh, whiche evermore him besieth and travayleth right sore my name to encrese (wherfor al that willen me good owe to do him worship and reverence bothe; trewly, *his better ne his pere in scole of my rules* coude I never fynde)—he (quod she) in a tretis that he made of my servant *Troilus*, hath this mater touched, and at the ful this question assoyled. Certaynly, *his noble sayinges can I not amende*; in goodnes of gentil manliche speche, without any maner of nycetè of storiers imaginacion, *in witte and in good reson of sentence he passeth al other makers*."'

Of course, no man could write such words of himself. But as most readers never succeeded in wading so far through the treatise as to reach the third book, the fancy

H

arose that it was written by Chaucer; and Godwin, in what can only be described as his comic Life of Chaucer, looked upon the whole as a piece of autobiography. However, the true meaning of this passage was dwelt upon by Hertzberg in 1866[1], and it has never since been included in the canon.

Several years ago, I observed that the first letters of the chapters formed an acrostic, and produced the following sentence :—MARGARETE OF VIRTW, HAVE MERCY ON THSKNVI ; and the treatise itself explains that MARGARETE OF VIRTW means Margaret endued with divine virtue, and refers either to the grace of God, or to the church. The last word I took to be the author's name, apparently transposed, but I could not explain it any further.

Meanwhile Mr. Bradley had satisfied himself that the author was probably Thomas Usk, who was politically somewhat conspicuous in the years 1384–8. He was further of opinion that the nonsensical name was due to some transposition in the text. Carefully perusing it with this idea, he noticed several distinct breaks in the sense, due to a dislocation of the text produced by a shifting about of the leaves of the MS. Having noticed these breaks, he proceeded to *rearrange* the text so as to better the sense ; and he had the great satisfaction of finding that the re-arranged text gave the last word as THINVSK, easily resolved into the *two* words THIN VSK (thine Usk)[2]. This at once settled the question, and at the same time explained why I failed to obtain the name by transposing the letters. It never occurred to me that the seven letters formed *two* words, and not one only.

For some account of Thomas Usk, see Walsingham's History, The Rolls of Parliament, and (in particular) the continuation by John Malverne of Higden's Polychronicon,

[1] Lounsbury, Studies in Chaucer, i. 201.
[2] See Mr. Bradley's letter in The Athenæum, Feb. 6, 1897.

ed. Lumby, vol. ix. pp. 45–6, 134, 150, 169; cf. Lingard, 1874, iii. 163–7. We can now determine, approximately, the date of the piece. Usk was executed on March 4, 1388; and we find him referring to past events that happened towards the end of 1384 or later. The most likely date is about 1387. For further particulars, see Ch. Pieces, pref. pp. xxi–xxxi.

It follows that both Troilus and The Hous of Fame were written before 1387, as we know to have been the case. For Usk coolly appropriates more than forty lines of The House of Fame, which he reproduces in prose without a word of acknowledgment; Bk. ii. ch. 2. 45–81.

**85. The Plowmans Tale;** ab. 1395. (Ch. Pieces, no. II. p. 147.)

This piece first appeared as a supplementary Tale in Thynne's second edition, in 1542. No MS. is known; and Thynne did well to preserve it, though it is highly probable that he was chiefly moved to print it because its religious views were likely to be extremely popular[1].

It must have been obvious to purchasers of Thynne's volume that this Tale was not seriously considered as belonging to the Canterbury Tales or to Chaucer; for it was added at the end, supplementally. But when, in the later editions of (about) 1550 and 1561, it was made to precede The Parson's Tale, and so thrust in amongst the rest, the idea that it was Chaucer's was easily suggested, and no less a person than Dryden accepted it as such[2].

[1] It had previously been printed *separately* by T. Godfray in folio, without date, but about 1532–5, probably under Thynne's care. From this separate edition (of which the only remaining copy, formerly Askew's, Farmer's, and Heber's, is now at Britwell) it was reprinted in W. Thynne's second edition of Chaucer's Works in 1542, and separately in octavo by W. Powell, about 1547–8.— H. Bradshaw (in Thynne's *Animadversions*, p. 101.)

[2] Lounsbury, Studies in Chaucer, iii. 108; cf. i. 183, 460. In the edition of (about) 1550, the first line of the Persones Prologue was

However, it was decisively rejected by Tyrwhitt (Introductory Discourse, § xl), who says, in plain words—'as
I cannot understand that there is the least ground of
evidence, either external or internal, for believing it to be
a work of Chaucer's, I have not admitted it into this
edition,' i. e. his edition of 1775. Every subsequent writer
has acquiesced in this decision.

For indeed, it is well known that the author of The
Plowman's Tale was the very man who, but a short time
previously, had written the celebrated alliterative poem
entitled Pierce the Ploughman's Crede, quite a distinct
work from that by William Langland. The author tells us
the fact himself, in The Plowman's Tale, l. 1065 :—

> ' Of freres I have told before
> In a making of a Crede—'

and the statement is strongly supported by internal evidence, since many striking words and phrases are common
to the two poems. Indeed, the Plowman's Tale itself is
strongly marked with alliteration.

Further, the following approximate dates cannot be far
wrong. The Crede, which (as the author remarks) is all
about the orders of friars, alludes, in l. 657, to certain recent
proceedings against one Walter Brute, which lasted from
Oct. 15, 1391, to Oct. 6, 1393, when he submitted himself
to the bishop of Hereford. We may well date the Crede
about 1394, and the Tale (which probably soon followed it,
as the author repeats many of its expressions) about 1395.

**86. The Praise of Peace**; by JOHN GOWER; 1399.
(Ch. Pieces, p. 205.) Found also in the 'Trentham' MS.

As this piece is headed—'Iohn Gower vnto the worthy
and noble kynge Henry the fourthe'—there is no more to

---

altered from ' By that the *Manciple* had his tale ended' to ' By that
the *Ploweman* had his tale ended'; a deiiberate and intentional
falsification of the text, contradicted by all the MSS.

be said. Not only Thynne, but every one who opened his volume, must have known positively that it was not written by Chaucer. The date is 1399, a little before Chaucer's death. Gower survived till 1408.

It is to be particularly noted that, if the inclusion of a poem in Thynne's Collection means that it is thereby 'attributed to Chaucer,' it must logically follow that such is the case with The Praise of Peace.

**87. THOMAS HOCCLEVE.** Two poems by Hoccleve must here be considered.

(*a*) **The Letter of Cupid ;** 1402. (Ch. Pieces, no. V. p. 217.) There are at least nine MSS.

This poem is now well known to be Hoccleve's, on MS. authority. That it is not Chaucer's, appears from the fact that it was not written till 1402, or after his death. The date is given in the two concluding lines of the poem :—

'The yere of grace joyful and jocounde
A thousand and foure hundred and secounde.'

(*b*) **To the kinges most noble grace ; and to the Lordes and Knightes of the Garter;** ab. 1415. (Ch. Pieces, no. VI. p. 233.) Found in MS. Phillipps 8151.

This piece was appended to the Table of Contents prefixed to Thynne's first and second editions and to the edition without date. It really consists of *two* Balades, but they were written at the same time. The former is addressed to King Henry V, and the latter to the Knights of the Garter. The probable date is 1415. That it was written by Hoccleve appears from its being placed among his poems in the Phillipps MS. no. 8151 ; and the same MS. has the heading—'Cestes Balades ensuyantes feurent faites au tres noble Roy Henry le quint (qui dieu pardoint !) et au tres honourable conpaignie du Iarter.'

It is obvious that a piece addressed to Henry V cannot be Chaucer's. See Hoccleve's Works, ed. Furnivall, p. 41.

**88. John Lydgate.** Several poems by Lydgate appeared in Thynne's Collection. I take them in the order in which they there stand.

(*a*) **The Flour of Curtesye**; ab. 1401. (Ch. Pieces, no. IX; p. 266.) No MS. is known. A poem of 270 lines, in thirty-eight 7-line stanzas, followed by an Envoy of four lines, which presents the earliest known example of the stanza employed by Gray in his Elegy.

Not attributed to Lydgate in edd. 1532, 1542, or 1550. But in 1561 Stowe reprinted it, and added to the title—'made by Ihon lidgate.' What authority he had for this we do not know, but the suggestion is obviously correct. That it is not Chaucer's, appears from ll. 236–8 :—

> 'Chaucer is deed, that hadde suche a name
> Of fair making, that [was], withoute wene,
> Fairest in our tonge, as the laurer grene.'

It follows that Thynne was perfectly well aware that it was not Chaucer's; yet we are asked to believe that everything which he included was thereby 'attributed' to that great poet.

That it was written very soon after Chaucer's death is highly probable, i. e. about 1401. See Schick, Introd. to Lydgate's Temple of Glass, p. c.

(*b*) **The Complaint of the Black Knight; or, The Complaint of a Loveres Life**; ab. 1402. (Ch. Pieces, no. VIII; p. 245.)

There are at least seven MS. copies. In one of these (Arch. Seld. B. 24) there is a colophon which assigns to it an entirely erroneous title :—'Here endith the Maying and disporte of Chaucere.' But fortunately, there is a copy in MS. Addit. 16165 (B. M.), in the handwriting of John Shirley, who took so much pains to find and copy out poems by Chaucer and others, in which he has this note :—'And here filowing begynnethe a Right lusty

amorous balade, made in wyse of a complaynt of a Right
worshipfull*e* Knyght that truly euer serued his lady, en-
duryng grete disese by fals envye and malebouche : made
by Lydegate.' On some of the pages is the heading :—
'The Compleynte of a Knight made by Lidegate.' The
five other MSS. are F., B., T., D., P. (See Appendix.)

As this ascription is commonly accepted, further discussion is hardly necessary ; yet it is interesting to note how
easily the rime-tests dispose of it. I mention a few.

(1) In the very first stanza it rimes *whyt-e* with *bright-e*
and with *night*.

(2) It presents mere assonances ; as *forjúged, excúsed*,
274 ; *wreke, clepe*, 284.

(3) The author confuses words in -*y* with words in -*yë*.
Exx. *pitously, malady(e)*, 137 ; *felyngly, malady(e)*, 188.

(4) He drops the essential final -*e* at the end of a weak
pt. t. Ex. *I ment* for *I ment-e*, riming with *diligent*, 246.

(5) He drops the final -*e* in *peyn-e*, which in Chaucer
is dissyllabic. Exx. *agayn, payn*, 233, 650 ; *seyn, payn*,
568. Also in *quen-e*. Ex. *queen, seen*, 674.

(6) He drops the final -*e* of the present tense, and of the
infinitive mood. Exx. *why, cry(e)*, 450 ; *diurnal, fal(le)*, 590.

(7) He rimes the short open *o* with the long one ; *sŏre*,
*tŏre*, 218.

(8) He rimes the long open *e* with the close *e*. Exx.
*grene, clène*, 125 ; *rède, spede*, 596. And confuses both of
these with a short *e* ; *wrĕche, lèche, séche*, 471.

Is it not enough ?

Schick dates this piece about 1402, after The Flour of
Curtesye, and before The Temple of Glass ; Introd. to
Temple of Glass, p. c.

(*c*) **A Ballad in Commendation of our Lady.** (Ch.
Pieces, nos. X and XI ; pp. 275, 281.)

This article, as printed by Thynne, consists of two
distinct and independent poems, as I was the first to

discover, by help of the MSS., viz. MS. Ashmole 59 and Sloane 1212. Yet the distinction is very marked. The former poem is addressed to the Virgin Mary, is of a religious tone, and is strongly marked by the use of alliteration; the latter is addressed to an earthly lady, is complimentary in its address, shows no marks of alliteration, and only appears in Thynne's edition, not in the MSS. above mentioned.

As to the former, it is thus headed in MS. Ashmole 59 :—'A devoute balade by Lidegate of Bury, made at the reverence of oure lady, Qwene of mercy.'

MS. Sloane 1212 contains an additional stanza, which I was the first to print; it also supplied several corrections.

It is obviously Lydgate's, though I can assign no date to it.

It presents a mere assonance in *piscyne, abyme,* 134. We also find the infinitive *telle* cut down to *tel,* in order to rime with *Gabriel,* 101 ; and the short *e* rimed with a long one, *wrĕche, lĕche,* 41. All three of these peculiarities occur in The Complaint of the Black Knight; cf. p. 103, (6) and (8).

(*d*) **To my Soverain Lady.** To the second poem, as it had no title, I assigned, as a heading—'To my Soverain Lady.' As it was printed in connexion with the poem just discussed, we should expect it to be Lydgate's; a notion which the internal evidence confirms. It is remarkable for containing eight entire lines in French; and my impression is that it was a complimentary Valentine addressed to Queen Katherine, wife of Henry V, who would, at any rate, have understood the French part of it, such as—*J'ay en vous toutë ma fiaunce.*

It is especially interesting from the fact that, in l. 21, it quotes the first line of 'Merciless Beautè.'

Short as it is, it contains one form for which the reader may search all Chaucer's works in vain, viz. *slo,* to slay, riming with *a-two*; for Chaucer's form is *slee.* We do indeed find the rime *two, sloo,* C. T., A 3245; but *sloo* in that passage happens to mean 'a sloe,' as again in R. Rose, 928. Cf. p. 81 (l. 15).

Lydgate, in l. 17, adopts Chaucer's Kentish form *knette,* for the sake of a rime to *besette.*

No MS. copy is known, as has already been stated.

(*e*) **Go forth, King.** (Ch. Pieces, no. XXIII; p. 408.) I know of no MS. copy of this poem.

This is a short poem of two stanzas only, or fourteen lines. It was first printed by Wynkyn de Worde about 1498, at the end of Lydgate's Temple of Glass. It is not thereby 'attributed' to Lydgate, but the internal evidence points strongly that way. At any rate, there is no pretence for ascribing it to Chaucer.

Do Chaucer's lines usually run like these?

> Womanheed, to chastitè ever enclyne.
> Be rightwis, jugë, in savíng thy name.
> Rich, do almesse, lest thou lese blis with shame.
> People, obey your king and the lawe.
> Trew servant, be dredful, and keep thee under awe.
> Inobedience to youth is utter distruccioun.

For *Rich,* Chaucer's form is *Rich-ë*; for *lese,* his form is *les-ë*; for *Trew,* he has *Trew-ë.* So far from improving the lines, such changes make them much worse, as any one can judge for himself. Surely it is not merely lawful, but advisable and meritorious, to apply such simple tests.

(*f*) **A Ballad of Good Counsel.** (Ch. Pieces, no. XII; p. 285.) There are at least two MSS.; Ff. and H.

In edd. 1532, 1542, and 1550, this piece has no title. But in Stowe's edition of 1561 the title is:—'A balade of good counseile, translated out of Latin verses in-to Englishe, by dan Ihon lidgat cleped the monke of Buri.'

It is eminently characteristic of Lydgate's style; and I suppose that no one disputes it.

At l. 79, *hardy* is made to rime with *foly*(*e*) and *flatery*(*e*). These are the chief poems by Lydgate that appear in Thynne ; but two more are discussed in §§ 93 and 95. Others were inserted at a later date ; see §§ 100, 102, 104, 105.

**89.** HENRY SCOGAN. **A Moral Balade** ; ab. 1406. (Ch. Pieces, no. VII ; p. 237.) There are at least two MSS. ; A. and H.

This piece is expressly assigned to Scogan by Thynne, and had previously been printed as Scogan's by Caxton. Thynne did quite right to insert it, because Scogan quotes the whole of Chaucer's 'Gentilesse' in ll. 105–25.

In l. 65 it is implied that Chaucer was dead.

**90.** SIR RICHARD ROS. **La Belle Dame sans Mercy** ; ab. 1450. (Ch. Pieces, no. XVI ; p. 299.) There are at least three MSS. ; F., Ff., and Harl. 372.

Tyrwhitt pointed out that the author's name is given in the Harl. MS. 372 ; where it is said to be 'translatid out of Frenche by Sir R. Ros.' And further, that it could not be Chaucer's, because the French original was written by Alan Chartier, who was only fourteen years old at the time of Chaucer's death.

It was first printed by Pynson, in 1526, in company with The Hous of Fame, &c.; hence its appearance in Thynne's edition. See Chaucer's Works, vol. i. p. 28.

**91.** ROBERT HENRYSON. **The Testament of Cresseid** ; ab. 1460. (Ch. Pieces, no. XVII ; p. 327.)

Even Thynne and Stowe must have known this poem to be other than Chaucer's, as they printed it in a spelling abounding with Scottish forms. An edition was printed at Edinburgh in 1593. L. 64 runs thus :—'Quha wait gif all that Chauceir wrait was trew ?' It is clear that no such line could have emanated from Chaucer himself. I know of no MS. copy ; but it is not unlikely that one (or more) may be found.

**92.** CLANVOWE. **The Cuckoo and the Nightingale** ;

ab. 1403. (Ch. Pieces, no. XVIII; p. 347.)   There are at least five MSS.; F., B., T., Ar., and Ff.

The question as to the authorship of this pleasing poem is now definitely settled, on the authority of the best MS. copy; and would have been settled long ago had that MS. been consulted. For at the end of the poem is written, in firm clear characters and by the same scribe— **Explicit Clanvowe.** See MS. Camb. Ff. 1. 6.

The title ' Of the Cuckoo and the Nightingale' is that given in Thynne's edition, and is suitable enough; but it is *not* the title given in the MSS. MS. Fairfax 16 and Bodley 638 give the title as ' The Boke of Cupide, god of Love.' As this title is evidently imitated from Hoccleve's ' Letter of Cupid, god of Love,' called in the Fairfax MS. ' Litera Cupidinis, dei Amoris,' we see that the author was acquainted with Hoccleve's poem, and probably wrote about 1403, or at any rate soon after 1402, which is the known date of The Letter of Cupid.

Again, the metre of the poem, which is very unusual, is obviously imitated from Chaucer, who, however, only once employed it, in the very last lines which he is known to have written. It is the metre of the Envoy to the Compleint of Chaucer to his Empty Purse; and we know that this Envoy was written in the autumn of 1399.

We should expect to find that Clanvowe was acquainted with Hoccleve; and it is on record that Sir John Clanvowe and Thomas Hoccleve are mentioned together in a document dated 1385; but this Sir John died in 1391. But the writer may very well have been Sir Thomas Clanvowe, who was a well-known character at the court of Henry IV, and a friend of 'prince Hal,' whom he had accompanied in the mountains of Wales. His name occurs in 1401 (Acts of the Privy Council, ed. Nicolas, temp. Hen. IV, p. 162), in 1404 (Testamenta Vetusta), and in 1406 (Wylie, iii. 207), and his will was proved in 1410 (ibid.).

This enables us to explain the reference to the queen at Woodstock, in l. 285. She was Joan of Navarre, prince Henry's stepmother, married to King Henry IV on Feb. 7, 1403; and it was she who received the manor and park of Woodstock as part of her dower. On March 15, 1411, she granted them to Thomas Chaucer (the poet's son) to farm; see Wylie's History of Henry IV for further details.

The above circumstances show that the poem was not Chaucer's, but it was not unnatural that it should have been printed in company with his works, as it is one of the best of the once 'doubtful' poems, and was written soon after his death.

The internal evidence against it does not amount to much; still it exists. In l. 52, the *e* of *assay-e* is wrongly suppressed, to gain a rime with *day* and *May*. The dissyllabic *gren-e* is cut down to *green* in l. 61, in order to rime with *been*. And the form *mon* replaces Chaucer's *man* in l. 85, in order to rime with *upon*.

The word *grede*, to cry out (135), does not occur in Chaucer. The Clanvowes came from Wigmore, in Herefordshire.

But the poem is quite *unique* in its use of the final -*e*. The author rather avoids elisions than otherwise, and hence the final -*e* occurs with far greater frequency than in any other poem of the same period.

That the author had read Chaucer, and aspired to imitate him, appears from his choice of metre, and from the fact that the first two lines of his poem form a quotation from the Knightes Tale (A 1785-6).

The date of the poem was certainly later than Feb. 7, 1403, but probably not much later. And it must be earlier than 1410. The poet professes to relate a dream which he dreamt on the third night of May (l. 55). At the time of writing, he was 'old and unlusty' (l. 37).

# CHAPTER X

**93.** So far is Thynne from 'attributing' poems to Chaucer, that he expressly does so in four instances only; in three of which he is right. The instances are :—

1. A goodlie balade of Chaucer.
2. The Dreame of Chaucer. [Book of the Duchesse.]
3. Good Counsayle of Chaucer. [Truth.]
4. Chaucer vnto his empty purse.

In the first case, however, he is mistaken. See Ch. Pieces, no. XXII, p. 405.

The piece really consists of *three* Balades all addressed to the same lady, named Margaret; and each Balade must have originally consisted of the usual three stanzas of seven lines each. But a stanza of the second Balade has been lost, so that there are eight stanzas in all instead of nine. An Envoy of eight lines is appended.

No MS. copy is known, so that Thynne's print is the only authority.

The internal evidence shows that it is almost certainly Lydgate's; no one now claims it for Chaucer.

It does not satisfy all the rime-tests. In the first Balade, the dissyllabic words *alle, calle, apalle, befalle,* are shortened to *al, cal, apal, befal,* to rime with *shal* and *smal.* The fifth stanza is too clumsy, both in metre and expression, to be considered as being in Chaucer's manner.

**94. The Assembly of Ladies.** (Ch. Pieces, no. XXI ; p. 380.) There are at least two MSS. ; Trin. and Addit. 34360.

I have shown strong reasons for believing that this poem was written by the authoress of The Flower and the Leaf. Yet it is remarkable that those who wish to claim the latter for Chaucer show no disposition to claim the former, no doubt because it is more prolix and in a less happy vein. But the critic must do one of two things; he must either prove them to be unconnected, or he must treat both alike. If he accepts one, he must accept the other. Both are quite distinct, in style and treatment, from all other poems of the fifteenth century.

These two poems are remarkable as being the two earliest poems in English which are claimed by a woman. A little later, we come to another, the famous Nut-brown Maid, which was almost certainly written by a woman, as is implied in ll. 22 and 177. It would be simply absurd to suppose that a fifteenth-century male poet would give himself out to be a woman; for he would only have been laughed at. The Tale of the Wife of Bath is not a case in point; every one understood what was meant.

The close connexion between the two poems will be considered when we come to examine The Flower and the Leaf.

The authoress declares herself in the first stanza; she says that she met four ladies, and was herself the fifth. In l. 370, a lady named Countenance appears, who calls them also 'sisters'; so again in l. 450. As no one now claims this poem for Chaucer, I omit further discussion of it here.

It fails to satisfy the rime-tests over and over again. In fact some of the rimes can only be described as bad. Such are : *doon* (done), *wone* (wont, custom), 2 ; *gyse*, *fantasy-es*, 9, which only rime by dropping the final *e* in

*gyse*, and the *e* in *fantasyes*; &c. At l. 48, *grene*, with close
*ē*, rimes with *clène*, with open *ē*; and so on. The reader
who knows anything of Chaucer's habits will easily detect
more examples.

Still more serious is the loss of syllabic -*e* in the middle
of a line, because this appeals even to the beginner. It is
not uncommon. Thus, l. 2 is as follows :—

'The fresh sesóun was altogider doon.'

It scans well enough, but the grammar is at fault. Chaucer
would have written *The fressh-e*, as a dissyllable. Compare—
'Right as *the fressh-e*, *red-e*, ros-e new-e';

Parl. Foules, 442.
'*The fressh-e* knight, the worthy man of armes';

C. T., F 1092.
Indeed, Chaucer uses *fressh-e* (without *the*) with a fem. sb. :
'And *fressh-e* Beautee, Lust, and Iolitee';

Pity, 39.

**95. A Praise of Women.** Probably by Lydgate.

It begins—'Al tho that liste of women evil to speke '—and
consists of twenty-five stanzas of seven lines each. It is not
reprinted in my Chaucerian Pieces, as it is of small interest.
The only MS. copy is a very poor one, in the Bannatyne
MS., fol. 275, written in 1568; which was printed for the
Hunterian Club in 1873–9; see p. 799 of that edition.
Thynne's text is reprinted in Morris's Chaucer, vi. 278; and
in Bell's Chaucer, 1878, iv. 416, where it is placed among
the 'Poems formerly attributed to Chaucer.'

It fails to satisfy the rime-tests in the following instances.
The infin. *ly-e* is cut down to *ly*, to rime with *sy* (saw),
134; and *quen-e* becomes *queen*, to rime with *been*, 160.

We find the rimes *y-bŏre* (born), *sōre* (sore), 16; *forlŏre*,
*yōre*, 158. The word *sere*, various, 72, does not occur
in Chaucer.

It was decisively rejected from the canon by Tyrwhitt, and it is hard to tell why Bell and Morris revived it.

In all the black-letter editions, the title is 'The Praise of Women.' The poem is eminently characteristic of Lydgate, and we may particularly observe the announcement of his intention to write a poem upon this subject, as stated in The Temple of Glas, 1378 :—

'I purpose here to maken and to write
A litel tretise, and a processe make
*In pris of women*, oonli for hir sake,
Hem to comende, as it is skil and right,
For here goodnesse, with al my ful[le] myght.'

I know of no reason why the poem here discussed may not be the 'litel tretise' here alluded to. No other such poem is known.

**96. The lamentatyon of Mary Magdaleyne.**

This piece, containing 102 7-line stanzas, had been previously printed by Pynson in 1526, in company with the Hous of Fame and some other poems, including La Belle Dame. It was decisively rejected from the canon by Tyrwhitt. It is thoroughly discussed in a dissertation by Bertha M. Skeat, Ph.D. (Zürich), printed at Cambridge in 1897; who gives many examples of instances which fail to satisfy the grammatical and metrical tests. There is even one example of assonance ; *disguysed, to-ryved*, 171 ; other notable rimes are those of *hue* (Ch. has *hew-e*) with *Jesu*, 674 ; *kene* with *eyen*, 127 ; *dy(e)* with *why*, 86 ; *hens* (Ch. has *henn-es*, hence) with the Latin pres. part. *liquescens*, 146 ; &c. She concludes :—'there seems every reason to suppose that this poem was written by a woman, who was also a nun'; and observes that the style of The Flower and the Leaf 'has nothing whatever in common with that of the pale dreamer of the Magdalene's sorrows.' A close examination of the language suggests 'the period

1460-1480 as the approximate date of the poem.' No MS. copy is known.

**97. The Remedy of Love.** Printed in Chalmers' British Poets, i. 539. In eighty-one 7-line stanzas, nineteen of which form a Prologue. The language is very late, that of the *sixteenth* century ; the probable date is about 1530. It contains such words as *incongruitie, deduction, allective, can't* (for *cannot*), *scribable* (fit for writing on), *olibane, pant, babé* (baby), *cokold* (which in Chaucer is *cok-e-wold,* tri-syllabic), *ortographie, ethimologie, ethimologise* (verb) ; also the Northern word *lait,* to seek. Twelve stanzas are occupied with a metrical translation of Prov. vii. 6-27.

How can we pretend that Thynne confined himself to printing genuine poems by Chaucer, when we find him thus inserting a poem which he must have known to have been written in his own lifetime? No MS. copy is known, or is likely to be found.

**98. Envoy to Alison.** (Ch. Pieces, no. XIX. p. 359.) The title is mine. It has hitherto been usual to print this piece *without any title,* as if it belonged to The Cuckoo and the Nightingale, which it happens to follow in Thynne's edition, and with which it has no connexion whatever. It also happens to follow The Cuckoo in MS. Tanner 346, but in MS. Fairfax 16 the two poems are a long way apart. It is really a Balade in the usual form, consisting of three 7-line stanzas, with a 6-line Envoy. It forms the dedication of a book, which the author (who ought to know best) addresses as—'O lewde book, with thy foole rudenesse.' If the book was no better than the dedication, we may congratulate ourselves on its loss. The initial letters of the lines in the Envoy form an acrostic, and give ALISON as the name of the lady to whom the book was addressed.

The Envoy affects grandiloquence, containing as it does the words *Aurore, Lucerne, Illumined,* and the line—'Sus-piries which I effunde in silence.'

The earliest known example of *effund* is dated 1420. The New English Dictionary quotes the above example as—'*about* 1500. *Cuckow and Night*. Lenvoye.' Of course '*Cuckow and Night*' is incorrect, but it is indeed difficult to tell what else was to be said; for, before the appearance of my edition, it was the only way of indicating where the word occurs. The assigned date, about 1500, is somewhat too late, as it occurs in the Fairfax MS. (ab. 1450).

I think the first four lines of the Balade are certainly imitated from the Envoy to Hoccleve's De Regimine Principum.

**99. A Ballad of good Counsel.** By Lydgate.

In the earlier editions it has no title; but in Stowe's edition the title is—'A balade of good counseile translated out of Latin verses in-to Englishe, by dan Ihon lidgat cleped the monke of Buri.' It begins—'Consyder wel [with] [1] euery cyrcumstaunce'; and consists of seventeen 7-line stanzas.

This piece has already been noticed in Chapter IX (p. 105), among the poems by known authors. It is obviously Lydgate's; and therefore not Chaucer's. It is printed in Chalmers' Poets, i. 555.

Thynne's book concludes with a Latin epitaph upon Chaucer, in thirty-four elegiac lines, by Stephen Surigon of Milan. It had previously been printed by Caxton at the end of his (separate) edition of Chaucer's Boethius [2].

**100.** Besides the pieces already discussed, Thynne also added three more pieces at the end of the Table of Con-

---

[1] I supply *with* from MSS. Ff. (Camb. Ff. 1. 6) and H. (Harl. 2251).

[2] Caxton concludes his edition of Boethius with a reference to Chaucer, 'of whom the body and corps lieth buried in thabbay of westmestre beside london to-fore the chapele of seynt benet, by whos sepulture is wreton on a table honging on a pylere his Epytaphye, maad by a poete laureat, whereof the copye followeth,' &c.

tents, viz. (1) Eight goodly questyons, with their answers; (2) Hoccleve's two Balades, discussed in § 87 (*b*); (3) Sayings (14 lines). It remains to discuss the first and third of these articles.

**Eight Goodly Questions;** printed in Bell's Chaucer, 1878, iv. 421.

In nine 7-line stanzas. There are two MS. copies; one in the Trinity MS., marked R. 3. 15; and another in the Bannatyne MS., printed by the Hunterian Club in 1873, p. 123. The latter helps us to correct *tree* (19) to *cofre*, which gives the right rime. This piece is merely expanded from the first seven lines of a poem by Ausonius, printed in Walker's *Corpus Poetarum Latinorum*, with the title Eorundem Septem Sapientum Sententiae.

It is quite in Lydgate's style, and may possibly be his. I suppose no one would take it to be Chaucer's.

However, in st. 5, the words *chastitee* and *honestee* are made to rime with the infinitive mood of the verb ' to lie,' as if it were *lee*[1]! But Chaucer's form is *ly-e*, dissyllabic, and with a different long vowel. Rime-tests are sometimes extremely useful and decisive.

**Three Sayings.** These lines had been previously printed by Caxton; and I have reprinted them twice; see Chaucer's Works, i. 46; vii. 450. And in the same, vii. pref. p. lxxxi, I have printed a similar Saying to the first one from MS. Ashmole 59, fol. 78. I now add, as a matter of curiosity, another variation found on an old detached fly-leaf of a MS., which was kindly lent me by Mr. F. W. Burgess, of Ringmer, Sussex, in 1898.

> ' Qwen p*r*estis faylin i*n* her sawes,
> And lordis turnin godes lawes
> Ageynis ry*ch*t[2],

---

[1] It is correctly spelt *lee* in the Bannatyne MS.
[2] Obviously an error for *skille*, i. e. reason.

And leccherie is holden as priuy solas,
And robberie as fre purchas,
Be war þanne of ille.
Than shal þe lond of albion
Turnin to confusion
As sumtyme it befelle[1].
*Ora pro anglia, sancta maria ;* quod Thomas cantuarie[2].'
This turns out to be the identical version printed (from
the same fly-leaf) in Sir H. Nicolas's edition of Chaucer,
and reprinted by Bell and Morris.

There is yet another version of these Sayings, with a note
that they would come true in 1461, in MS. Dublin (Trin.
Coll.) E. 5. 10. See Thynne's *Animadversions*, ed.
Furnivall, p. xlvi. They are therefore older than that year.

These popular sayings were associated with Chaucer
merely by the accidental circumstance that they were
printed by Caxton at the end of his edition of Chaucer's
Anelida and Complaint to his Purse in order to fill up
a blank space.  Discussion is needless.

**101.** THE UNDATED EDITION. There is but one undated black-letter edition of Chaucer, and the date of it is
about 1550.  Book-catalogues frequently call it the 'second '
edition, in order to enhance the price; but it certainly
appeared *after* 1542, as the spelling is throughout distinguished by the introduction of numerous additional
misprints, as already exemplified at p. 95.  It agrees with the
edition of 1542 in all other respects, except that it places
the Plowman's Tale before the Parson's, an arrangement
which is preserved in the later editions of 1561, 1598, 1602.
and 1687.

[1] Read *befil*.        [2] Referring to Thomas à Becket.

# CHAPTER XI

## STOWE'S EDITION

**102.** In 1561 appeared a reprint of the third or undated edition (of about 1550)[1], to which numerous additions were made by John Stowe. Most of these, but not all, were spurious. The volume deserves particular consideration.

In the first place, happening to have room for just three stanzas in the second column of fol. cccxxxii, back, at the end of Gower's Praise of Peace, Stowe inserted three separate poems, each containing a single stanza of seven lines. To these he gives the following titles :—

1. A saiyng of dan Ihon.
2. Yet of the same.
3. Balade de bon consail.

I have reprinted them in Chaucerian Pieces, no. XV. p. 297. I know of no MS. copy.

Observe that Stowe expressly attributes the first two to Dan John, i. e. to Lydgate ; and we may fairly do the same with

---

[1] Certainly from that particular edition. The Prologue to the Plowman's Tale is exactly reprinted from the edition of 1542 in Thynne's *Animadversions*, ed. Furnivall, p. 101. The same is reprinted from Stowe's edition [wrongly called by me, alas ! 'an early undated edition'] in my notes to Pierce the Ploughman's Crede, E. E. T. S., p. 45. I compare these with the third or undated edition, and find that the readings in Stowe certainly follow that edition, not that of 1542. Cf. Chaucerian Pieces, p. xv (footnote), where ' fol. xc' and 'fol. xciii' should be transposed. See § 81, p. 95.

regard to the third, in which *losse* (loss) rimes with *crosse* (cross). In Chaucer, the MSS. sometimes have *cros*, but commonly *crois* or *croys* ; and the latter represents Chaucer's pronunciation, as he twice rimes it with *voys* (voice), C. T., B 451, C 532. Hence none of these three is Chaucer's.

I take occasion to note that the first two stanzas are on the same theme, and translate a medieval proverb, which is given in MS. Fairfax 16, fol. 195, in the form—'Quatuor infatuant, honor, etas, femina, uinu*m*.' A third version of the same proverb occurs in the second stanza (omitted by Stowe) of 'O Mossie Quince.' See § 105, p. 124.

**103.** However, Stowe was successful in finding a few genuine poems, and this encouraged him to subjoin about a score of pieces, with the following preliminary adver-tisement :—' Here foloweth certaine woor*kes of Geffray Chauser, whiche hath not here tofore been* printed, and are gathered and added to this booke by Ihon Stowe'; and again, on fol. ccclv, back, is the colophon :—

'Thus endeth *the workes of Geffray Chaucer.*'
To which he appended Surigon's Latin epitaph on Chaucer, and Lydgate's Siege of Thebes ; and of course he knew this to be Lydgate's, as the author announces his name in l. 92 of the prologue.

The genuine pieces, which need no discussion, are these :—

**A balade made by Chaucer**, teching what is gen-tilnes. This was not really new, as it had previously been quoted *in extenso* in the poem by Henry Scogan (§ 89).

**A Prouerbe** [*read* Prouerbs] against couitise and negligence. Commonly called 'Proverbs'; see Ch. Works, no. XX; vol. i. p. 407. As these consist of only eight short lines, and are commonly accepted, they need not be discussed. Cf. § 53, p. 61, note 1.

**A balade whiche Chaucer made agaynst women vnconstaunt.** See § 55, p. 62.

These verses next folowing were compiled by
Geffray Chauser, and in the writen copies foloweth
at the ende of the complainte of petee. This testimony is of some importance. The poem in question is
'A Compleint to his Lady.' See above, § 53, p. 60, note 1.

Chaucer's Woordes vnto his owne Scriuener; also
called Chaucer's Wordes unto Adam. See above, § 53.

It is worth observing that Stowe expressly attributes all
these poems, except the eight lines of Proverbs, to Chaucer.
In the poems which we have still to consider, he does this
only twice. See §§ 104, 105 below.

**104. Beware of Doubleness.** The first spurious piece
is entitled:—'A balade whiche Chaucer made in the praise
or rather dispraise of women for ther doublenes.' See
Ch. Pieces, no. XIII. p. 291.

Stowe is here certainly mistaken; for there are four fair
MSS. of it, in three of which, viz. Fairfax 16 (fol. 199),
Ashmole 59, and Addit. 16165, it is expressly attributed to
Lydgate; and the two last of these MSS. belonged to
Shirley, who is much to be depended on. It is in Lyd-
gate's best manner, much smoother than his wont, and
I have nothing to say against it as a composition. Still, it
is not Chaucer's.

In the second stanza, it fails to satisfy the rime-tests.
The dissyllabic words *grene, wene, mene,* are docked of the
final *-e* in order to rime with *seen.* N.B. The fourth MS.
is Harl. 7578.

**Chastity.** It is convenient to consider next the poem
numbered 58 in Ch. Works, i. 34, printed in Stowe at
fol. cccxlv, back (misnumbered cccxxxix). It is headed:—
'A balade declaring that wemens chastite Doeth moche
excel all treasure worldly.' It begins—'In womanhede as
auctours al write'; and extends to nine 7-line stanzas
(sixty-three lines).

The final *-es* only occurs once, in *nobl-es;* the final *-ed* would appear to be thrice fully sounded, but five times reduced to *'d*; the final *-en* occurs but thrice, and the final *-e* not at all, unless it be in *poor-e*. In other words, it is much later than the time of Lydgate, and helplessly remote from the time of Chaucer. And it is but a poor performance. It is printed in Chalmers' English Poets, vol. i. p. 565. I am not acquainted with any MS. copy.

**105.** The remaining pieces, all spurious, were simply pitchforked into the volume because Stowe had access to the MS. which contained them. Fortunately, the MS. is still accessible, being now in the library of Trinity College, Cambridge, where its class-mark is R. 3. 19; and the inspection of it throws much light upon Stowe's methods. It is remarkable that he only claims *one* of these poems for Chaucer; even his hardihood could go no further. The poem in question is the following :—

**The Craft of Lovers**; Trin. MS., fol. 156. Stowe's heading is:—'This werke folowinge was compiled by Chaucer, and is caled the craft of louers.' It consists of twenty-three 7-line stanzas (161 lines), and is printed in Chalmers' English Poets, vol. i. p. 558, with a footnote to the effect that 'Ritson attributes this to Lydgate.' But it seems too bad even for Lydgate, and the ascription of it to Chaucer is so preposterous as much to discredit Stowe's judgement.

In the 23rd stanza the date of the poem is thus exhibited in the Trinity MS. :—

> 'In the yere of our lorde a .M. by rekeninge
> CCCCXL .&. VIII. yere folowing.'

So that, according to the MS., the date is 1448. But as this was inconsistent with the editor's assertion in the title, he judiciously omitted a C, and so reduced the date to 1348, when it is doubtful whether Chaucer was more than eight years old.

There are at least two other MS. copies, very closely

resembling one another, viz. MS. Addit. 34360 and Harl.
2251; but they exhibit the date somewhat differently. The
former has :—

> 'In the yeere of god . a mł by Rekenyng
> Foure hundred fifty and .ix. yere folwyng.'

With this the Harl. MS. agrees, giving the date as 1459;
which is more probable. In any case, we are clear as to
the century.

The first line of the poem appears in a startling form, as
to which the copies substantially agreè. MS. Addit. 34360
has it thus :—

> 'To moralise a similitude who list these balett*is* sewe.'

It is clear that 'a similitude' was once a marginal note,
which has crept into the text. The first two stanzas are
introductory. The next twenty stanzas are spoken alternately
by a man and a woman, named respectively Cupido and
Diana in the Addit. MS. The 23rd stanza is there headed
'Conclusio'; but this MS. and the Harl. MS. alike add
a 24th stanza, headed 'Verba auctoris.' As this has not
been printed, I give it here, to show the kind of stuff that
'was compiled by Chaucer':—

> 'Go, litel balett*is*, submyttyng eue*r*ywhere
> To due correccion of benyuolence;
> But where that envye is, com[1] nat there
> For anythyng; kepe your balett*is* thens.
> For envy is ful of froward reprehens,
> And how to hurt lyth eue*r* in a-wayte;
> Kepe ye thens, that ye be nat ther bayte[2].'

The remaining poems are mostly beneath discussion;

---

[1] Harl. loke ye come.   But this is little better.

[2] There are two more stanzas, but I think they belong to another
poem.   The *former* of them (as Tyrwhitt remarks) is printed by
Stowe elsewhere, viz. at the top of col. 1 of fol. cccxliv.

they nearly all belong to the middle of the fifteenth century.  I give their names.

A **Balade**; Trin. MS., fol. 156, back.  Begins—'Of their
nature they greatly the*m* delite.'  In four 7-line stanzas (twenty-
eight lines).  The second stanza quotes the line—'Be ware
alwaye, the blind eateth many [a] flye'; which forms the
refrain of the Balade warning men against deceitful women;
for which see p. 124 below.

**The .x. Commaundements of Loue**; Trin. MS., fol.
109.  Begins—'Certes, ferre extendeth yet my reason.
In fourteen 7-line stanzas (ninety-eight lines).  In the last
stanza, the author describes himself, with perfect truth, as
being 'a man unknown.'  However, there is a copy of the
poem in MS. Fairfax 16, so that it is as early as 1450.

**The .ix. Ladies worthie**; Trin. MS., fol. 110, back.
Begins—'Profulgent in preciousnes, O Sinope the quene.'
In nine 7-line stanzas (sixty-three lines); one stanza for
each lady.  For the list, see Ch. Pieces, p. xiii.

[**Virelai**.]  From the Trin. MS., fol. 160; see Ch.
Pieces, no. XXV. p. 448.  This piece has *no title* either
in Stowe or in the MS.; the name 'Virelay' in Moxon's
edition was due to a remark by Tyrwhitt, who cautiously,
or perhaps incautiously, spoke of it as being 'perhaps by
Chaucer,' and said that 'it comes nearer to the description
of a *Virelay* than anything else of his that has been preserved.'  But this is incorrect; see note to Anelida,
l. 256; in Ch. Works, vol. i. p. 536.

To attribute it to Chaucer is impossible, from the nature
of the case.  For each line consists of *four* syllables only,
the forty lines having the rimes thus arranged : *a a a b a a a b :
b b b c b b b c : c c c d c c c d : d d d e d d d e : e e e f e e e f.*  But in
Chaucer's language many of these lines would have *five*
syllables, as—'And sor-ë sighing'—'Out of mesur-ë'—and
so on; and some of the rimes would become no rimes,
viz. such as *lat-e*, adv. (dissyllabic), *hat-e* (dissyllabic), *what*

(a monosyllable) ; *certain, peyn-e.* Finally, the rime *find-e, end-e,* is indefensible, unless the author pronounced them as *find, ind,* riming with *wind.* Probably the poem is in the East-Anglian dialec̄t. It contains the interesting word *ure,* destiny, which is common in Barbour, but occurs also in Lydgate and Skelton (both East-Anglians) and in The Court of Love, written by a clerk of Cambridge.

A Ballade ; Trin. MS., fol. 160. It begins—' In the season of Feuerere, when it was full colde.' In seven 7-line stanzas (forty-nine lines). In praise of the daisy, and very poor. Some of the lines seem to have six accents. Chaucer would not have rimed *rèd-e* (red) with *Margarete* !

A Ballade ; Trin. MS., fol. 161. In twelve 7-line stanzas. The Trin. MS. has thirteen stanzas, but Stowe omitted the tenth, because it coincides with st. 19 of the Craft of Lovers. It is made up of scraps from other poems. Stanzas 1–4 form part of a poem on the fall of man, from Lydgate's Court of Sapience. It begins—' O mercifull and o merciable.' In st. 8 occurs the assonance of *hote* (hot) with *stroke* ; and in st. 9, that of *cureth* with *renueth.*

The Judgement of Paris ; Trin. MS., fol. 161, back. Stowe's heading is—' Here foloweth how Mercurie with Pallas, Venus, and Minarua (*sic*) appered to Paris of Troie, he slepyng by a fountain.' In four 7-line stanzas (twenty-eight lines) ; apparently incomplete. It is but a poor performance.

A Balade plesaunte ; Trin. MS., fol. 205. Begins— ' I haue a Ladie where so she bee.' In seven 7-line stanzas. Meant to be facetious ; e. g. ' Her skin is smothe as any oxes tong.' Imitated from Lydgate's poem entitled A Satirical Description of his Lady, in Lydgate's Minor Poems, ed. Halliwell, p. 199. The author says that when he was fifteen years old, he saw the wedding of queen Jane ; and that was so long ago that there cannot be many such as himself still alive. As Joan of Navarre was married to Henry IV in 1403, he was born in 1388, and would have been sixty-two in 1450. This gives us a likely date for these precious productions.

**An-other Balade** ; Trin. MS., fol. 205, back. Begins—'O mossie Quince, hangyng by your stalke.' In four 7-line stanzas, of which Stowe omits the second, though it is less scurrilous than the other stanzas. It runs thus:—

> 'Wyne, women, worshyp, vnweldy age
> Make men to fonne, for lak in theyr*e* resons;
> Elde causeth dulnesse and dotage,
> And worship chaunge of condicions;
> Excesse of wyne blyndeth theyr*e* dyscrecions;
> And all*e* book*es* that poet*es* made and radde
> Seyen women most make men madde.'

Two of Lydgate's stanzas are on the same theme. See § 102, p. 118.

**A balade, warnyng men to be ware of deceitptfull** (sic) **women** ; Trin. MS., fol. 207. See Ch. Pieces, no. XIV. p. 295. In seven 7-line stanzas; with the refrain—'Bewar therfore; the blind et [*eats*] many a fly.'

This is much the best of these poems, and is probably Lydgate's, being, indeed, in his most characteristic style. There is a better copy in the Trinity MS. marked O. 9. 38, with a unique additional stanza, so that the poem really consists of seven stanzas, as said above, though Stowe prints but six, as in his MS. There is yet another copy in MS. Harl. 2251, which contains a large number of Lydgate's poems. It was attributed to Lydgate by Tyrwhitt, who refers us to this MS.; but I do not find Lydgate's name against this poem in particular, though the poem which follows it is so marked. Note that in the Trinity MS. it is *preceded* by a well-known poem of Lydgate's, written as a satire upon the extravagant 'horns' then worn by ladies. Why Stowe omitted that poem it is difficult to understand, as he prints some that precede it, and one that follows it.

**The Court of Love.** This poem occurs quite at the end of the Trinity MS., in a later hand of the sixteenth century. So much has been made of this pleasing but much over-rated poem that it will be discussed separately, in the next chapter.

**106. Praise of Chaucer.** There is yet one more poem printed by Stowe and due to this seductive MS., viz. the single stanza which he inserted at the end of Thynne's portion of the volume, by way of a finale, with the title— 'A balade in the Praise and commendacion of master Geffray Chauser for his golden eloquence'; from the Trin. MS., fol. 25. See Ch. Pieces, no. XXIX. p. 450. It begins—' Maister Geffray chauser, that now lithe in graue. It occurs, in the MS., at the end of a copy of The Parlement of Foules. In Stowe's edition, it is printed on fol. cxxxvii, back.

**107.** One rather wonders what happened to this book of Stowe's, as the foliation, near the end, is so eccentric. After fol. cccxxxvii (ending Thynne's portion) comes fol. cccxl. After fol. cccxliv, which ends the extracts from the Trinity MS. (with the sole exception of the Court of Love), comes fol. cccxxxix, containing a genuine poem by Chaucer (A Complaint to his Lady) and one other piece of which the last two lines run over on to the next folio, where (together with the word *Explicit*) they are crowded up so as to occupy only half an inch. And this next folio, on which the Court of Love begins, is called fol. cccxlviii. That is to say, fol. cccxxxviii is replaced by *five* leaves, the first of which is misnumbered cccxl in unusually small type, whilst the other four leaves contain pieces *all* óf which are from the Trinity MS. Then comes fol. cccxxxix, as if only *one* leaf had originally intervened after fol. cccxxxvii. And lastly, when we come to The Court of

Love, it is at fol. cccxlviii, as if several leaves had been taken out. It looks as if some special manœuvring took place at the last moment, in order to include the poems from the Trinity MS.; and some further contrivance was again necessary, in order to include The Court of Love.

**Chance of the Dice.** I take the opportunity of mentioning here a poem which Stowe attributed to Chaucer, though it is included neither in his edition of 1561, nor in Speght's edition of 1598.

Professor Hales kindly refers me to the passage in Stowe's Survey of London descriptive of St. Andrew's Undershaft, the church in which, by the way, Stowe was himself buried; see the reprint of the Survey by Thoms, p. 54.

'Geoffrey Chaucer, writing of a vain boaster, hath these words, meaning of the said shaft: —

Right well aloft and high ye beare your heade,
The weather-cocke with flying as ye would kill;
When ye be stuffèd, bet of wine then brede,
Then lookè ye, when [that] your wombe doth fill,
As ye would beare the great shaft of Cornehill.
Lord! so merily crowdeth then your crok[k]e
That all the streete may heare your body clok[k]e.'

A marginal note by Stowe says—'CHAUCER, *Chance of Dice.*' I have succeeded in identifying the above passage. It is the sixth stanza of an anonymous poem entitled *Chance of the Dice*, extant in MS. Fairfax 16, fol. 194. The MS. supplies the word *that* in l. 4, and gives the reading *floon*, i. e. 'arrows,' in place of the nonsensical *flying* in l. 2. It also corrects *croke* and *cloke* to *crokke* and *clokke*. *Crowdeth* means 'presses forward'; *crokke*, 'crock,' i. e. round paunch; *clokke*, 'cluck,' make an inarticulate noise (N. E. D., s. v. *Cluck*, verb (2), § 3). The poem is certainly not Chaucer's, but it may be Lydgate's.

# CHAPTER XII

## THE COURT OF LOVE

**108.** It is only by an abuse of language that The Court of Love can be said to be 'attributed to Chaucer.' We have seen that even Stowe hesitated as to whether he ought to insert pieces from what is now the Trinity MS., and when he came to The Court of Love, written in the handwriting of his own age, he seems to have hesitated again. He was doubtless strongly influenced by the fact that he had really discovered the unique copy of an unprinted and meritorious poem; and considering the very large number of non-Chaucerian pieces which he had already admitted into his volume, we can hardly wonder that he finally decided upon giving the world the benefit of his discovery. And in fact, he did quite as well in printing this poem, as in adding Lydgate's Siege of Thebes.

Rightly understood, the association of this poem with Chaucer amounts to no more than this; that, when Stowe was reprinting for the fourth time a collection of Middle-English poems, containing most of Chaucer's genuine works together with a still larger number composed by numerous other poets, he thought well to take the opportunity of publishing an unknown poem of which he had fortunately secured the sole copy. And that is all that can be said.

**109.** It is singular that the possibility of the genuineness of this poem is still somewhat despairingly clung to; for the case against it is of exceptional clearness. It has been well stated by Prof. Lounsbury in his Studies in Chaucer, i. 497; from whom I quote a few sentences:—

'The evidence against its being a work of Chaucer's is overwhelming. It fails, in the first place, to conform to every test that has been laid down. It rymes together constantly words belonging to the groups designated by their endings in -*yë* and -*y* and -*e*. It surpasses "The Flower and the Leaf" in the extent to which it rymes words that grammatically have different terminations. Of the two hundred and six stanzas of which it consists, there are more than thirty cases in which the sense is carried on from one to another. . . The very names of two of the characters, Philogenet and Philobone, point to the composition of the poem as belonging to a period when the study of Greek was reviving in the west, and that did not even begin till after the capture of Constantinople in 1453. . . . The grammar of the poem proves beyond question that it does not belong to the fourteenth century. On this point there can be no difference of opinion among students of English. . . . The peculiarity about this poem is that it has a modern grammar with an archaic vocabulary, and the vocabulary has at times been borrowed without its being thoroughly comprehended.'

Professor Lounsbury proceeds to insist on the extreme rareness of the use of the words *do, doth, did,* as mere auxiliaries in writings of the fourteenth century; and adds—'Such forms as *do hight* (145), *doth stik* (675), *doth shine* (787), *doth wryte* (798), *doth hew* (980), *doth plese* (1008), *doth stere* (stir, 1068), *doth bete* (beat, 1090), *doth unshit* (unshut, 1245), and *doth purvey* (1396) occurring in a poem of fourteen hundred lines, would be hard to explain, even were there evidence of no other kind to meet. . . . But one instance—the preterite *did honge*—is to be found in "The Flower and the Leaf" (245).'[1]

He also notices the failure of the author in his attempts to imitate archaic diction; remarking—'He was trying to do earlier what Spenser tried to do later. This much can be said for him, that the latter failed more signally than he.'

**110.** As my object is less to furnish the full proof of this matter than to enable the reader to prove it for himself, I shall indicate the methods to be used without pressing home every point. Unless the student does some of the work for himself, he will never comprehend the full force of the arguments, but will probably underrate them unduly. The point is, that The Court of Love hopelessly fails to meet most (though not all) of the various tests. We will try some of them in order, beginning with § 28 in Chapter III.

**111. Final -es.**

1. Final *-es* marks the *gen. case sing. of substantives.* Examples in The Court of Love: *quen-es*, 104, 292; *king-es*, 126, 272; *lov-es*, 91, 179, 191; *wight-es*, 312; &c. This suffix lasted long as an archaism, and was well understood; cf. *night-es starres*, in Sackville's *Induction*, st. 9.

2. *The plurals of substantives.* Ex. *flour-es*, 5; *term-es*, 15; *drop-es*, 22; &c. Examples are numerous; but the suffix lasted long, and is common in Hawes. The plurals *stones*, 77, *sterres*, 82, seem to be monosyllabic. The pl. *estat-es*, 84, is suspicious; for Chaucer has *estats*[2].

3. *The adverbial suffix.* Ex. *none.* On the other hand, The Court of Love has *hens*, 739, 1326; *hensforth*, 289;

---

[1] I observe five instances in The Assembly of Ladies, 6, 41, 195, 466, 590 (*not* 569); but it is both longer and later than The Flower and the Leaf. The Court of Love (with ten examples) is less than twice as long.

[2] I do not give references to Chaucer, as they can be found in my Glossarial Index.

K

*ons*, once, 994; *thens*, 1269; *whens*, 905; and in 931, *ellis* is really *els*. This direct contradiction to Chaucer's grammar is extremely serious.

**112. Final -en.** The author of The Court of Love practically makes this suffix take the place of Chaucer's final *-e*. Unluckily, he introduces it not only where it is correct, but where it is not.

4. *The infinitive mood.* Ex. *writen*, 35, *maken*, 81, *byden*, 189, *stiren*, 324, *beten*, 324, *quyten*, 327, *sweren*, 509; &c. In at least *some* of these cases Chaucer would have used *-e*.

5. *The gerund.* Ex. *to dressen*, 179; *byden*, 321, *semen*, 607, *holden*, 683, *shewen*, 784, *seken*, 838, *laughen*, 1011; cf. 1165, 1186, 1335.

6. *The pp. of a strong verb.* Ex. *holden*, 62; *shapen*, 136, 816, 1354; *growen*, 182; *yeven*, 547, 742; *dronken*, 998; *blowen*, 1240. But all these forms lasted till late, and some are still in use.

7. *Plural of the present tense.* Ex. *taken*, 10, *wailen*, 256, *foten*, 586, *speden*, 945, *approchin*, 1212, *singen*, 1384, *rejoisen*, 1435. With *we*: 1153, 1155, 1405; with *ye*: 958, 999. *Plural of the past tense.* Ex. *spakin*, 624; cf. 822, 1208, 1375. In at least *some* of these cases, Chaucer would have used *-e*; but our author does not seem to have known this.

8. *Prepositions.* Ex. *withouten*, 125, 187, 249, 317, 486, 959. *Adverbs*: none.

The above references record only the author's successes; his failures are far more numerous, as he frequently forgets to add either *-en* or *-e*; these failures will be noted below in § 103. I will only observe here that *he did not know* that the final *-en* had any etymological value in the prep. *withouten*; hence he actually has *withóut*! See ll. 320, 740, 979. He even has *without*, accented on the former syllable!! See l. 69.

On the other hand, the fictitious character of the final *-en* appears from the fact that it is exhibited in wholly impossible forms. It would be difficult to match, from any author, the following utterly disgraceful specimens :— that thou serven, 290; that she me helden, 347; to tyme [i. e. until] thou seen, 499; thay kepten been, 526; I kepen, 684; if this mater springen out, 725; if that I . . greven, 928; that god hath . . leften, 1166.

**113. Final -e** ; cf. §§ 30–34.

9. *Substantives of A. S. origin.* Ex. *none.* Why is this? Why are *tong(e)*, 807, *ster(re)*, 580, *hart* (for *hert-e*), 635, 717, 1090, mere monosyllables?

10. *Substantives of ' F.* origin. Ex. *none.* But why not? Why are *best(e)*, 594, *fest(e)*, 1425, monosyllabic?

11, 12. *Datives and genitives.* Ex. *none.* On the other hand, where Chaucer has *herte rote*, our author has *hartes rote*, 1263. For how could he have known that *herte* might represent a genitive?

13. *Adjectives of A.S. origin.* Ex. *none.*

14. *Adjectives of F. origin.* Ex. *none.*

15. *Adjectives ; plural.* Ex. *none.*

16. *Adjectives ; definite.* Ex. *in thilkë place*, 642; *his lenë bodie*, 1257; cf. *prymèrose*, 1437. Not enough for so long a poem ; the number of failures is large ; ex. *her hygh*, 7; *the fresh*, 231; *the first*, 304; *the thrid*, 316; *the fourth*, 323; *the fifth*, 330; &c.

17. *Verbs ; the infinitive.* Ex. *none.* We actually find *passe*, 329, *reyve*, 331, *tell(e)*, 343, &c., treated as monosyllables.

18. *The gerund.* Ex. *to dred-e*, 603; *to serv-e*, 909. Not enough. Cf. *dy'*, 317, *ples'*, 471, &c., &c.

19. *Pp. of a strong verb.* Ex. *none.* Cf. *withhold'*, 991, *begon'*, 1064, &c.

20. *Pt. t. of a weak verb.* Ex. *none.* But we find *led* for *lad-de*, 219, *caught'*, 218, *dred* for *drad-de*, 771, *gret* for *grette*, 772, &c.

21. *Other verbal inflexions.* Ex. *none.*

K 2

**22.** *Adverbs and prepositions.* Ex. *amidd-e*, 188. Not enough ; cf. § 112 (8).

Surely the failures are most conspicuous; it needs no specialism to see them. And they abound.

**114.** But the fact is simply, that the author knew no more about Chaucerian grammar than if he had been born in the sixteenth century, so that when we come to investigate his rimes from this point of view, his blunders are distressing. He did not know that the final -*e* had a grammatical value, so that, in l. 13, when he rimed *write* with *aright*, he not only ignored the guttural *gh*, but he rimed *aright* (without a final -*e*) with the infin. *writ-e* or *wryt-e*, in which a final -*e* is grammatically essential. The blunders of this sort are numerous ; but I purposely give only the references ; for the student may learn more by finding out what is wrong for himself than he can learn by having all the details explained. If, for example, he examines l. 65, he will see that *wend* and *frend* are, in Chaucer (see Glos. Index), respectively *wend-e* and *freend*, which give no rime. The references are : 65, 86, 121, 128, 149, 188, 216, 225, 251, 359, 400, 407, 408, 440, 456, 457, 468, 491, 517, 522, 527, 534, 566, 580, 587, 643, 652, 727, 736, 751, 762, 797, 800, 809, 842, 863, 895, 951, 1038, 1049, 1063, 1077, 1108, &c.

**115. Rime-tests.** See Ch. IV. §§ 38–46. It is absurd to suppose that a late poem of this description can conform to rime-tests. But it is best to be remorseless ; so I proceed.

**Rimes in -y and -yë.** These endings are, of course, jumbled together. Ex. descry(e), hy, 97 ; verily, signify(e), 102 ; I, dy(e), 212 ; I, espy(e), 282 ; and see 298, 405, 419, 695, 704, 1014, 1138, 1147, 1152, 1348, 1420[1].

---

[1] I give only the references ; partly to save space, and partly because the student should really do just a little of the work for himself. –He has only to refer to my Glossarial Index. I give the number of the *former* of the lines to be compared.

**Rimes in -ight, -yt.** These are likewise mixed pp.
Ex. write, aright, 13; delyt, hight, 144; delyt, sight, 4§2;
bright, whyte, 790; delyt, knight, 870.

**Open and close o.** See § 40. Our author seems to
keep these apart; but, though he succeeds in this respect,
he rimes *doon* with *son-e* thrice, 155, 272, 944. And the
rime of *pore*, to pore upon, with *colóur*, 1273, is abnormal.

And I take occasion here to notice his rime of *environ*
(Chaucer, *enviroun*, riming with *adoun*, Leg. 300) with *ôòn*,
one, 1031. Much worse is that of *opinion* with the pp.
*begon* in l. 1063, because Chaucer's forms are *opinioun*
and *begon-ne*. Equally extraordinary is that of *nonne* (a nun),
1149, with *boun*, a Northern abbreviation of *bound* or
*bounden*; because Chaucer's forms are *nonne* (nun·nə) and
*bound-en* or *bound-e*.

**Open and close e.** See § 45. These are usually
distinguished; yet we find the rime of *grene* (A.S. *grēne*),
green, with *clène* (A.S. *clǣne*), clean, 816.

**116.** Even the above difficulties are not all. There
still remain to be explained away such rimes as *kepe, flete,*
309, which is a mere assonance; *eke, lyke,* 561; *lyke, stik,*
673; *plaint, talént,* 716; *offencion, begon* (Ch. has *offencioun,
began*), 921; *eloquence, hens* (Ch. has *eloquenc-è, hennes*),
933; *opinion, begon* (already noted), 1063; *frend, mind,*
1056; *company, destinè,* 1170; *here, desire,* 1301. Worst
of all is *here, grene,* 253; yet the text looks correct. A
*very* moderate acquaintance with Chaucer will soon demonstrate that he perpetrates no such offences as these[1].

**117.** If we try to obtain positive evidence as to what
the poem really is, it is not too much to say that the

---

[1] One ought almost to draw a veil over such examples of 'grammar'
as *thou wot*, 1045; *thou can*, 462; and the grotesque change of
*counterpleted be* to *counterpleted indede* in l. 429, which is stolen from
Ch. Leg. 476.

evidence strictly limits it to the very end of the fifteenth century or the beginning of the sixteenth.

The New English Dictionary will one day enable us to test its *vocabulary*. We can already do so to some extent; for it is surprising how many words appear in this poem for the first time. I note, for example, the *earliest dates* which the Dictionary gives as *other* examples of a word's appearance :—*demene*, demeanour, 734, and in More (A.D. 1534); *dulled*, 478, known in A.D. 1514; *bedreint*, 577, known in 1563; *flawe = flave*, yellow, 782, known in 1657; *directed*, 785 (instead of Chaucer's *direct*), known in 1598; *assomoned*, 170, known in 1594; *bass*, 797, known in 1529; *aureat*, 817, known in 1599.

The following examples are the earliest known (i. e. if the Court of Love be set aside) :—*aged*, 111, known in 1440; *as blife*, 161, found in Lydgate, ab. 1413; *absent (oneself)*, 190, found in Hoccleve, ab. 1420; *baleis*, 80, known in 1414; *acroke* ,378, used by Caxton; *cocold* (for Ch. *cok-e-wold*), 410, ab. 1530 (see p. 113); *to fon*, 458, known in 1440; *courtly*, in the sense of 'polite,' 474, known in 1460; *clenliness*, 475, found in Lydgate, ab. 1430; *celsitude*, 611, found in Dunbar, ab. 1500; *bay-window*, 1058, known in 1428; *patens*, 1087, known in 1440; *deformity*, 1169, used by Caxton, &c.

No example is known, in the fourteenth century, of *demure*, 653; *devoid of*, 667 (Rom. Rose, but in Fragment B, viz. in l. 3723); *a fig for*, 685; or of the phrase *to give a horn*, 1390. All these things require explanation. And what is meant by *dye and sterve*, 301 ?

Quite a beginner can see the difference between the *accentuation* of words here and in Chaucer. Cf. Ch. *désíróus*, C. L. *desírous*, 44; Ch. *withóut-en*, C. L. *wíthout*, 69; Ch. *óbeisáunc-ë*, C. L. *obeísance*, 213; Ch. *viság-e*, C. L. *vísage*, 224, 275; Ch. *condici-oun*, four syllables, C. L. *condícion*, three syllables, 259; so also *excepcion*, 261, *sup-*

*plicacion*, 977. Such changes are, at least some of them, of late date.

**118.** The *pronunciation* shows that the poem was written after the change of long *e* to its modern sound, which began in the North, but took time to reach the South. Hence *ee*, eye, rimes with *degree*, 132, and with *see*, 768; *company* with *destinè*, 1170; *yen = een*, eyes, with *lyne* (liin), 135; *here* with *desire*, 1301; and *eke* with *lyke*, 561, just as *fyne* rimes with *seen* in Sackville's Induction, st. 68. At l. 543, *reyve*, for *reve*, seems to be an alteration made for the sake of getting a rime to *deceive* and *gleyve*.

The smoothness of the metre, as compared with that of Hawes[1], is easily explained from the fact that the author was probably familiar with Scottish poetry, such as that of King James (whom he sometimes imitates), Dunbar[2], and others. A trace of this appears in the Northern form *me thinkes*, 874. But he was probably an East-Anglian; for we have traces of *-in* for *-en*, as in *spakin*, 624, and *approchin* and *bringin* in the same stanza, 1212, 1217; and we may note his use of the word *ure*, 634, 862, which occurs in Lydgate and Skelton and in Northern writers, and of the Northern *boun* for *bounden*, 1151; see N. E. D. His statement that he was 'of Cambridge, clerk,' 913, may perhaps be taken in the most literal sense.

The proof of the lateness of the date of The Court of Love is so complete that, owing to purely lexicographical facts, the editors of the New English Dictionary have found themselves compelled to adopt so late a date as c. 1530; as under *Horn*, 6. b. If it was inspired by the appearance of Thynne's Chaucer, the date is about 1533.

---

[1] Hawes seems to have copied Lydgate. But the poems of Surrey, Wiat, Higgins, and Sackville are reasonably smooth.

[2] Whence, probably, his *celsitude* and *pulcritude*, 611, 613.

# CHAPTER XIII

## ADDITIONS BY SPEGHT

**119.** Two reprints of 'Chaucer' were issued by Speght in 1598 and 1602. He professed to 'edit' the book; but he does not appear to have much improved the text by his alterations, which are sometimes right, and sometimes wrong. I give a specimen of each sort.

In the Prologue, l. 123, Thynne (1532) has:—

Entewned in her voyce ful semely—

which was reproduced in the later editions, until Speght altered *voyce* to *nose*; correctly.

In the same, l. 212, Thynne (1532) has:—

He had made ful many a maryage.

And here Speght altered *made* to *rid*; wrongly. See further in Lounsbury's Studies, i. 276. Speght also provided a Life of Chaucer, a list of his works, arguments to the poems, and a glossary. The glossary is a fine store-house of 'ghost-words,' and was largely drawn upon by Skinner, Kersey, and Bailey. Thus, where Chaucer has *farsed*, stuffed, in l. 233 of the Prologue, Speght gives it as *fassed*; this Skinner misread as *sassed* and then turned into *sased*, which he imagined to mean 'seised.' *Sased* is a ghost-word, having no real existence; and this is how such words are made. Coles, in 1684, gave: '*Sased*, stuffed'; showing that he knew the right sense required.

**120.** In the edition of 1598, Speght added but three

more pieces, all spurious; viz. Chaucer's Dream, A Ballad, and The Flower and the Leaf. He inserted them just after The Court of Love and before Chaucer's Words to Adam, in order that the latter poem might conclude the volume, i. e. not counting Lydgate's *Siege of Thebes*. For some mysterious reason, the *Ballad* is generally looked upon as being part of the *Dream*, though it is quite a distinct piece, and is separated from it by six lines, of no value, which have nothing to do with either the Dream or the Ballad!

**Chaucer's Dream.** This title was assigned to the poem by way of begging the question; for it is of later date than Chaucer's time. The proper title seems to have been *The Isle of Ladies*, which rightly describes it. There is (or was) a MS. of it at Longleat, written in the sixteenth century, about 1550, and another in the British Museum of about the same date, viz. MS. Addit. 10303. See Thynne's *Animadversions*, ed. Furnivall, p. 30, and Lounsbury's Studies in Chaucer, i. 482. It consists of 2206 lines[1], in the same metre as The Hous of Fame, and is printed in the editions by Chalmers, Moxon, Bell, and Morris. Tyrwhitt unluckily opined that it might be genuine, but no one now adopts this view. It is a case in which rime-tests are very useful, as the rimes are often truly astonishing and significant.

Thus the rime of *be* with *companie*, 107, 121, at once shows that the date is after the change of M.E. long *e* to the sound which it has at present; and this is clinched by the rimes of *grene* (better *green*) with *yene* (better *een*, i. e. eyes) at ll. 351, 1719; and of *nine* with *green*, 1861. We are far away from Chaucer when we find *queen* riming with *kneen*, pl. of *knee*, 293, 1779; for the Chaucerian

---

[1] In Morris's edition the lines are misnumbered. The reprints seem to be very incorrect.

forms are *quen-e* and *know-es*. And this is quite enough.
To find more such curiosities is an easy task. Indeed,
the very next rime to that of *green, een,* is formed with
the words *pleasaunce* and *fesaunce,* where *fesaunce* is a
playful way of spelling 'pheasants.'

But we can go further; for the Northern character of
this piece is somewhat strongly marked. Thus at l. 331, the
rime *stonds* (i. e. stands) and *londs* (lands) really indicates
that the forms are *stond-es, lond-es*; for the Southern and
Midland *stondeth* will not rime at all. At l. 323, we find
the rime of *know* with *low,* where *lowe* is a licentious
spelling of mod. E. *law*; hence the original rime was that
of *knaw* (or *knawes*) with *law* (or *lawes*); and *knaw* is
Northern. The Northern pres. part. in *-and* occurs in
*servand, livand,* 1629; and in *avisand,* riming with *hand,*
1883. Hence it is neither Chaucer's nor Lydgate's.
However, it is not Scottish, but only a northern form of
Midland; indeed, the author is not consistent throughout,
for at one time he has *goth* (goeth) riming with *wroth,*
785, and at another has *goes,* riming with *rose,* 1287, 1523.
Mere assonances sometimes occur, as in *undertakes, scapes,*
337; *remember, tender,* 1415. It bears no resemblance
whatever to Chaucer's poetry, and is really one of the
fifteenth-century romances. It should be compared with
Chestre's Sir Launfal.

**A Ballad.** Strictly speaking, there are *two* pieces here,
which are unconnected. The first is a very short and
worthless poem of six lines, consisting of three heroic
couplets (the third line having lost a word or two); whilst
the second is in the regular ballad form, consisting of three
7-line stanzas, with a refrain. But instead of an envoy,
there are merely these two lines, probably added by a later
hand :—

> 'Ye that this ballad redè shall,
> I pray you, keep you from the fall.'

The Ballad begins—'Go forth, myn ownè trewe herte innocent'; and the refrain is—'Give thee the blis that thou desirest ofte.'

I think this Ballad is of the early part of the fifteenth century, and is almost certainly Lydgate's.

These pieces are only connected with Chaucer's Dream by the accident that they occur in the same MSS.

**121. The Flower and the Leaf.** In eighty-five 7-line stanzas (595 lines). See Ch. Pieces, no. XX. p. 361. No MS. copy is known. This poem has so frequently been praised, that I feel some diffidence in saying that perhaps too much has been made of it. Still, this does not dispose of the fact that, like the Assembly of Ladies, it claims to be the production of a woman; nor of yet another fact that, whilst it is much superior to the Assembly of Ladies, it has so much in common with it that we cannot shut our eyes to the natural conclusion that the same authoress wrote both these poems. Both consist almost wholly of descriptions, and are wholly lacking in interesting touches of personal character. Whatever opinions they express are of a highly genteel and ladylike order.

It was doubtless attributed to Chaucer because he refers to the flower and the leaf (which seems to have been a common theme, touched upon also by Gower and by Eustace Deschamps) in his Legend, ll. 188–194. But it is remarkable that, while the authoress most distinctly pronounces in favour of the lasting leaf and against the fading flower, Chaucer is careful to say that he expressly declines to express a preference for one above the other. Cf. Lounsbury, Studies in Chaucer, i. 493.

The arguments against the genuineness of both these poems (for they stand or fall together) have been given at some length in my Chaucerian Pieces, pp. lxii–lxx. I merely give here a summary of them.

1. Nearly all the descriptions are characteristic of a

woman; there are minute references to colours, dresses, ornaments, and decorations. In both poems, the ladies vie with each other as to who looks the best (F. 188, A. 384; where F.=Flower, and A.=Assembly).

2. The two poems have many phrases, and even whole lines in common. I here merely point out *one* example.

' And forth they yede togider, twain and twain ' ; F. 295.

' See how they come togider, twain and twain ' ; A. 350.

3. Both use *very* with an adj., as in *very rede, very good*, F. 10, 33, 315; A. 479. This construction is found in Lydgate, but not in Chaucer.

4. There are abundant examples in which F. transgresses Chaucer's grammatical usages as explained in Chap. III. The use of the final *-e* is artificial, fitful, and capricious. It is regarded as ornamental, not as necessary to the grammar. This the reader can discover for himself, if he knows how to analyse the lines. For the information of beginners, I give the numbers of the lines where words that require *no* final *-e* are made to rime with those that do so. See the words that rime with those that terminate the following lines, viz. 16, 27, 30, 48, 62, 69, 74, 85, 90, 99, 106, 114, 130, 148, 162, 167, 174, 181, 188, 202, 207, 209, 212, 219, 230, 249, 260, 282, 298, 312, 324, 337, 347, 389, 398, 414, 417, &c. It is a pretty exercise for a novice to find out what is wrong; when in doubt, he can look out the words in the Glossarial Index to Chaucer. Thus, at l. 16, the rimes are *night, might, wight*; but, unluckily, *might* should be *mighte*.

5. But these errors are merely in final words. In the middle of a line, they are not infrequent. Thus l. 53 seems to run rightly :—' That most lyk tó green wol [*wool*], wot I, it was.' The accent on *to* is unpleasant; but the fatal error lies in *green*; for Chaucer's form is always the dissyllabic *gren-e*. The heroic remedy is to omit *to*; but this cannot be done in all such cases. Are we to omit

*fresh* in l. 109—'Wher shé sat in a fresh green laurer-tree'? Not so; for, at l. 249, *green* has to rime with the monosyllabic pp. *seen.*

6. The ignorance of Chaucer's grammar is very marked in such cases as *forshronk* as a pp., which ought to be *for-shronke*, 358; in the use of *rood* as a plural, instead of *riden*, 449, 454. Read *riden*, and then observe the resulting discord. In l. 282, *began* rimes with *man*; unluckily, *began* is a grammatical blunder for *begonne* (with *o*=short *u*). The form *ware*, meaning 'wore,' takes the strong form, 259, 261, 267, as in modern English; whereas Chaucer has the weak form *wered*.

7. Of course the endings *-y* and *-yë* are mixed up; see ll. 85, 106, 130, 162, 174, &c.

8. The rime of *be* with *pretily*, 89, points clearly to the fifteenth century.

9. The open *o* seems to be distinguished from the close *o* (as in modern English). But the open and close *e* are jumbled together twice. At l. 43, we find *brède*, breadth (A.S. *brǣdo*), *wede*, a weed (A.S. *wēod*); and at l. 289, we find *grene* (A.S. *grēne*), *clène* (A.S. *clǣne*).

10. These rimes are imperfect :—*note, sot*, 99; *orient, wante*, 148; cf. *be, pretily*, 89.

11. When all these things (and many more) have been explained away, what is to be done with ll. 519, 520?

> 'Eek ther be knightès *olde* of the Garter,
> That *in hir tymè* did right worthily.'

It is not a historical fact that Chaucer wrote many years after the order of the Garter was founded.

**122.** Speght brought out another edition in 1602, in which he added two more pieces, viz. *Jack Upland* and *Chaucer's A B C.* As the latter is genuine, it need not be discussed.

**Jack Upland.** This is an outspoken and rather fierce

attack upon the friars, written in prose in the form of questions, and is obviously not Chaucer's. It was at once replied to by one John Walsingham, who called himself Friar Daw Topias; whereupon Jack immediately issued a rejoinder, in which he refers to the recent seasonable hanging of some friars, which took place in June, 1402. Probably all three pieces belong to that year. The Reply of Friar Daw, and Jack's rejoinder, are printed in Political Poems and Songs, ed. Wright, ii. 16.

Speght was perhaps aware that Jack Upland had been previously printed. A copy exists in the library of Caius College, Cambridge, which seems to have been printed about 1536[1]; and though Speght's text occasionally differs from it, there may have been some intermediate edition. He may have introduced corrections in the few places where his text offers an improvement. On the whole, the earlier text is a better one. It is printed in Ch. Pieces, no. III. p. 191; and a facsimile of the title-page forms the frontispiece to the present volume. I have not succeeded in finding any MS. copy.

[1] It is bound up with another tract dated 1536, and printed in the same type and style. The title-page quotes a verse from Ezekiel xiii, as it stands in Coverdale's Bible (1535).

# CHAPTER XIV

## ADDITIONS BY URRY AND OTHERS

**123**. A reprint of Speght's edition appeared in 1687; but it need not detain us.

The next edition, by John Urry, in 1721, is the worst of the set. Urry had singular notions as to how Chaucer should be spelt, and it is both difficult and useless to discern his methods. But it is necessary to say that he added two new pieces to the pile; both of them undoubtedly spurious, though the first is of some importance, and both have a certain interest of their own. It is sufficient to give their names. They are :—The Tale of Gamelyn, and The Mery Adventure of the Pardonere and Tapstere, forming a prologue to The Merchant's Second Tale, or The Tale of Beryn, which is duly subjoined to it.

**The Tale of Gamelyn.** Though this tale is not by Chaucer, it belongs to his age. It is probable that he contemplated recasting it, and it would have made an admirable Yeoman's Tale. It is frequently found in a certain class of MSS. of the Canterbury Tales, where it occurs after The Cokes Tale; in consequence of which it has often been misnamed The Cokes Tale of Gamelyn. It is reprinted in my edition of Chaucer, in the Appendix to vol. iv. p. 645. I also edited it in a separate form, for the Clarendon Press, in 1884 (2nd ed. 1893).

**The Pardonere and Tapstere.** This is a somewhat jocose account of the doings of the pilgrims when they arrived at Canterbury, and it forms a Prologue to the Tale of Beryn. It consists of 732 long lines, and is obviously a supplement to the Canterbury Tales by a later hand.

**The Tale of Beryn.** This is a rather prolix tale, in 3292 long lines, imitated from an old French romance entitled L'Histoire du Chevalier Berinus. These two connected pieces are found in one MS. only of the Canterbury Tales, viz. the Duke of Northumberland's MS., no. 55, in which they are inserted after The Canon's Yeoman's Tale. It was printed from this MS. by Urry, and has since been re-edited, for the Chaucer Society, by Dr. Furnivall and Mr. W. G. Stone (1876–1887).

Vol. i of Chalmers' British Poets, printed in 1810, contains a very complete collection of all the works in any way associated with Chaucer, from the Canterbury Tales to the Tale of Beryn.

Tyrwhitt's edition of the Canterbury Tales, which appeared in five vols. 8vo. in 1775–8, and was reprinted at Oxford in two vols. 4to. in 1798, is a most valuable work, which will always retain a high place on account of the excellence of its Notes, Prefaces, and Glossary. His text is far better than that of any preceding edition ; and he did all that was at that date possible for the elucidation of his author. It is a matter for regret that his edition was limited to the Canterbury Tales alone, though his Glossary includes words from most of Chaucer's works.

There is a convenient reprint by Moxon, entitled ' The Poetical Works of Geoffrey Chaucer, with an Essay on his Language and Versification and an Introductory Discourse; together with Notes and a Glossary by Thomas Tyrwhitt.' Many have supposed this to mean that Tyrwhitt edited all the poems contained in the volume, which, from the nature of the case, is impossible. The Canterbury Tales alone are from Tyrwhitt's edition ; the other poems are mere reprints from editions in black letter.

**124.** In later editions still further additions were made. Thus in Bell's edition of about 1856 appeared the following :—

**Merciless Beautee ;** see above (§ 54). It had previously appeared, for the first time, in 1765, in Percy's Reliques of English Poetry. It is almost certainly genuine. From MS. Pepys 2006.

**Proverbs of Chaucer.** The first eight lines are genuine, and had been printed before ; see above, § 103. But two 7-line stanzas were appended by Bell, which are wholly unconnected with the 'Proverbs' and with each other, and are not Chaucer's. The former stanza, beginning—'The world so wyd, the eyre so remuable'—is the first stanza of a poem by Lydgate ; and the second stanza, beginning—'The more I go, the ferther I am behinde'—is likewise the first stanza of another poem by Lydgate. See MS. Harl. 2251, fol. 22, back, and fol. 37, back ; and Lydgate's Minor Poems, ed. Halliwell, pp. 193, 74.

Of the *former* poem there are other MS. copies, viz. in MS. Harl. 2255, fol. 14 ; MS. Rawlinson C. 86 (Bodleian) ; and MS. Q. Γ. 8, fol. 33, in the library of Jesus College, Cambridge. The mistake of putting these two detached stanzas together occurs in MS. Harl. 7333, where Shirley attributes them to one 'Halsam squiere'; he had perhaps seen a copy made by Halsham of these two stanzas, with his name appended to them, and erroneously supposed that it was the name of the author ; and the mistake is repeated in MS. Addit. 16165, as is more fully explained below.

The reason given by Bell for subjoining these stanzas is extraordinary. 'Only the first two stanzas are given in the printed editions ; but in the MSS. which have been consulted for the present text, the rest follow without any distinction.' As it is perfectly common for poems to follow one another in MSS. 'without any distinction,' the reason is in itself a weak one. But it loses all its force when we

L

find it to be only true in the case of *one* MS. out of three !
There are, in fact, but three MSS. which give the 'Proverbs' and the two stanzas, viz. Harl. 7578, Fairfax 16,
and Addit. 16155. In Harl. 7578 the stanzas follow on,
as stated, but in Fairfax 16 they immediately *precede* the
Proverbs; whilst in Addit. 16165 they not only precede
the Proverbs, but there are *two other pieces in between*. And
besides this, the last-named copy has, above the two stanzas,
this heading—'Two verses [i. e. stanzas] made in wyse of
balade *by Halsham esquyer*.' This is an excellent example
of the casual way in which 'Chaucer's poems' have been
dealt with.

**Orison to the Holy Virgin.** Begins—'Moder of god,
and virgin undefouled.' In twenty 7-line stanzas (140
lines). This piece also appeared in Bell's Chaucer, and the
reason for inserting it is easily discovered. It abounds
with Northern peculiarities, because it was taken from MS.
Arch. Selden B. 24, which contains a number of poems by
Chaucer *and others* in Scottish spelling. This is the very
MS. which also furnished the two pieces mentioned below,
named 'Prosperity' and 'Leaultè vault Richesse.' It so
happens that, at the end of the poem which we are now
considering, the Scottish scribe, who was not well informed
as to the authorship of poems by English authors, added
the note—'Explicit oracio galfridi chaucere.' However, it
is needless to discuss the question any further, for it is well
known that he must have made a mistake. The poem was
undoubtedly written by Hoccleve, and has been edited by
Dr. Furnivall from the Phillipps MS., which contains a
collection of Hoccleve's poems. See Hoccleve's Works,
ed. Furnivall, p. 52.

This piece had previously appeared in Leyden's edition
of The Complaint of Scotland, published in 1801.

In Morris's Chaucer, in six volumes, 1866, which was
to some extent a reprint of Bell's, the additional stanzas to

the Proverbs and Hoccleve's Orison to the Virgin were retained; and the following pieces were added :—

**Aetas Prima**; or, **The Former Age**. A genuine poem, found in two MSS. of Chaucer's translation of Boethius; viz. MSS. Camb. Univ. Library, Hh. 4. 12 and Ii. 3. 21.

**Prosperity.** A single stanza of eight lines. It is now known to have been written by John Walton, as it is really a stanza taken from his verse translation of Boethius, written in 1410; see Warton, Hist. Eng. Poetry, § 20. It is therefore not Chaucer's. It occurs in MS. Arch. Selden B. 24, fol. 119, where it is wrongly attributed to Chaucer.

**Leaultè vault Richesse.** Another stanza of eight lines, from the same MS., fol. 138. There is no reason for supposing it to be genuine; and two for supposing it to be otherwise. It contains *no* example of a final *-e* as constituting a syllable, and it rimes the pp. *lent* with the infin. *repent-e*. This and the preceding piece were here printed for the first time.

**125.** In my six-volume edition, Oxford, 1894, I added the following, some of them genuine, but the rest doubtful, though illustrative of Chaucer's 'Complaints.'

**Balade to Rosemounde**; Minor Poems, no. XII. Genuine; attributed to Chaucer in the unique MS. copy, in MS. Rawlinson Poet. 163, which also contains Troilus.

**An Amorous Compleint**; or **Compleint Damours**; Minor Poems, no. XXII. In thirteen 7-line stanzas, written at Windsor. External testimony is lacking; the internal testimony is somewhat in its favour. Cf. § 56. There are at least three MSS.

**A Balade of Compleynt**; Minor Poems, no. XXIII. In Chaucer's manner; but certainly an imitation. Cf. § 57. From MS. Addit. 16165, fol. 256, back.

**Womanly Noblesse.** Attributed to Chaucer by Shirley, in the MS. copy. In three 9-line stanzas, with a 6-line envoy; thirty-three lines on only three rimes. It is printed

as Minor Poem, no. XXIV, in vol. iv. p. xxv.  Cf. § 58.
From MS. Addit. 34360.

**Complaint to my Mortal Foe**. Printed as Minor
Poem, no. XXV, in vol. iv. p. xxvii. In four 8-line stanzas ;
reasonably correct as to grammar and rimes.  Cf. § 59.

**Complaint to my Lode-sterre**.  Printed as Minor
Poem, no. XXVI, in vol. iv. p. xxix.  In seven 7-line
stanzas.  Correct as to grammar and rimes, except that
*alas* rimes with *space*, usually *spac-e*.  The rime seems permissible, as in Sir Thopas the word *plac-e* rimes with *grac-e*,
but also appears as *plas*, to rime with *gras* ; B 1910, 1971.
And, in the ' Proverbs,' we find the rime of *embrac(e)* with
*compas*.  Cf. § 59.  The last two poems are certainly by the
same author.  They occur in MS. Harl. 7578, where they
immediately follow Chaucer's Complaint to Pity.

# NOTE TO CHAPTER VI

(See p. 74.)

**126.** THE latest criticism on Fragment A of the Romaunt of the Rose occurs in an article by Dr. J. Koch, in Englische Studien, vol. xxvii. pp. 61–73. It is much to be regretted that Dr. Kaluza, to whom we owe so much for his separation of Fragment A from the rest, has taken up the untenable position of claiming Fragment C for Chaucer, as well as Fragment A. Koch takes advantage of this at once, arguing that if Fragments A and C are by the same author, it is obvious that Chaucer wrote neither of them, because it is impossible that Fragment C can be genuine.

Koch further raises difficulties by attacking the rimes in Fragment A. To my mind, not one of these difficulties is fatal, so that the attack rather strengthens the case in its favour than otherwise. It is a tedious task to show this, as the charges are, many of them, frivolous. But it is necessary, I suppose, to perform this weary task. His objections are twenty in number, but are all inconclusive. The rimes objected to are as follows.

1. *Macrobes, lees*; l. 7. The form *Macrobes* is objected to, because we find *Macrobeus* in Book Duch. 284. But *Macrobes* is in the French text; and though it be true, as Koch points out, that the passage in the Book of the Duchesse refers to the very same original, Chaucer varies his proper names so much that nothing can be concluded

from his use of *Macrobeus*. Unless, indeed, we are to say that the Parliament of Foules is not his, because the form there used is *Macrobie* (l. 111).

2. *gay, hay*; l. 53. The pl. *hayes* is in Troilus, iii. 151; but the singular should be dissyllabic (*hay-e*); Fr. text *haie*. The form is uncertain; the A.F. form occurs as *le hay* as early as 1302-3, in the Year-books of Edward I, years xxx and xxxi, p. 173.

3-8. *gardyn, theryn*, 481; *ingyn, gardyn*, 601; cf. ll. 699, 1279, 1380. The objection is that Chaucer accents *gardyn* on the former syllable elsewhere. But we know how he vacillates between *sánguin* and *sanguýn*, *Aústin* and *Austýn* (B 1631), *Simkin* and *Simkýn* (A 3941), *Látin* and *Latýn* (A 638). Yet this counts as *five* difficulties!

9. *journée, she*; l. 579. Elsewhere Chaucer has *journey*, riming with *wey*, E 783 (once only). But it is *journey* that is exceptional; *journee* is in the Fr. text, and is etymologically correct. In A 2738, the five best out of the seven chief MSS. have *Iournee, iurne, Iourne*.

10. *pryse, deuyse*; l. 887. We should expect *preyse* (as in the Glasgow MS.), not *pryse*, as in Thynne. I do not know why; both *prize* and *praise* are in common use at this day; and the sb. *prys*, in the sense of 'price,' rimes with the sb. *devys* in A 815. The verbs *prysen* and *preysen* were somewhat differentiated in sense (see Prompt. Parv.); and *pryse* seems to suit the present passage. It is very common in Barbour.

11. *care, were*; l. 505. But here the reading must be wrong, whoever wrote the poem; for there is no rime at all. It is clear that emendation is required, and I still believe that the former line originally ended with *were*, i.e. defend (it), to translate the French *garisse*, to which it exactly corresponds. It is highly probable that a supposed 'correction' may have been made here by the Northern continuator, or author of Fragment B, in whose eyes the repetition of

*were* seemed meaningless, and for whom such a rime as *care, war,* would be good enough. That Fragment A, with its perfect Midland grammar, is not in the Northern dialect, must be obvious to all.

12. *shet, mette*; 1341. It is admitted that the text is here faulty, whoever wrote the poem; for it contradicts the very careful grammar found in the rest of the piece. Koch declares that the grammar is correct; i. e. that *shet* is the pp. of *shēten,* to shoot! But the pp. of *shēten* is *shoten,* and *shet* is the pp. of *shetten,* to enclose.

13. *been, wreen*; l. 55. Elsewhere, Chaucer has *wryen.* But *wreen* is a correct form; and two good MSS. have *wre* for *wrye* in Troil. ii. 380. We can conclude nothing certain from such things as these.

14. *ageyn, leyn* (gerund); l. 183. Elsewhere, Chaucer has *leye,* not *leyn.* But *leye* and *leyn* are equivalent; cf. *leyn,* pr. pl., H 222. Chaucer rimes *leyn,* pp. with *seyn,* E 2393; and *seyn* with *ageyn* only nine lines further on.

15. *pope-holy, prively*; l. 415. Here Koch coolly proposes to alter the 'unmeaning' word *pope-holy* to *papelardie,* merely because *papelardie* occurs in Fragment C, 6796 (by another author). The object, of course, is to try to establish a case in which a word in *-yĕ* rimes with a word in *-y*; precisely the very thing that does not occur in Fragment A at all. The unfortunate word *pope-holy* is called an obvious scribal error! But it was once rather a favourite word with our ancestors, as shown in my note to Piers Plowman, C. vii. 37. Strictly speaking, it is an adjective; but it could be used as a sb. also, as by Lydgate, Minor Poems, p. 46—'And for *popholy* and vyce loke wel aboute'—where it means 'hypocrisy.' That it was a popular corruption of *papelardie* is quite possible; if so, it is, all the more, the right word to employ here.

16. *sak, stak*; l. 457. Here *stak* is used intransitively; whereas Chaucer elsewhere uses it as transitive (see Troil.

iii. 1372). But why not? The author of *Pearl* has *stek*, pt. t. s. intransitive, Gawain, 152; and *steken*, pt. t. pl. transitive, Cleanness, 884. Chaucer himself uses *stikked* as equivalent to *stak* (transitive) in Legend, 2202; and makes the pp. *y-stiked*, A 1565. There is much confusion, in M.E., in such verbs as this, both as to form and usage; and it is remarkable that such a fact should evoke any surprise.

17. *flokkes, laverokkes*; l. 661. Elsewhere, we are told, Chaucer uses only the form *larke*, not *laverokke*. But why not *both* forms, seeing that *lark(e)* also occurs in Fragment A, l. 915? Of course, Chaucer must have been quite familiar with the form *laverok*; for it occurs in Gower, C. A. ii. 264.

18. *love, behove*; l. 1091. This, we are told, is a Northern rime, and therefore inadmissible. That it is not also a Southern rime has yet to be proved; at any rate, Gower rimes *behove* with *glove*, C. A. i. 15, *glove* being a perfect rime to *love* in modern English. And, in C. A. i. 215, he rimes it with *prove*. The fact is, that *behove* is quite an exceptional word, and frequently mispronounced; see the New Eng. Dictionary.

19. *wone, Rone* (or *woon, roon*); l. 1673. As we do not exactly know what *roon* means, we cannot conclude anything definite as to its pronunciation. The difficulty is discussed in my Glossarial Index, which was not consulted.

20. *aboute, swote*; l. 1705. Discussed above; see p. 79.

It will be seen by any one who cares to examine the above examples, that only in case no. 20 is any of the alleged objections final or decisive. They are quite of a different character from those which occur in the case of Fragment B or Fragment C. Indeed, those numbered 3–8, 12, and 15 are mere mistakes, and tell the other way. The impression which the above examination leaves upon my mind is that the objections practically fail.

**127.** Koch also raises the question of the vocabulary employed, but this is a very fallacious test, and quite indecisive. The famous Prologue is not to be rejected as spurious because it contains more than eighty words which occur nowhere else in Chaucer[1]. And it is not irrelevant to remark that the adj. *deliver* occurs only in Prol. 84, and in Rom. Rose 831 ; *pers* only in Prol. 439, 617, and in R. R. 67 ; and the adj. *tretys* only in Prol. 152, and in R. R. 932, 1016, 1216. The sb. *courtepy* occurs only in Prol. 290, D 1382, and R. R. 230; the adj. *fetis* or *fetys* only in Prol. 157, C 478, and in R. R. 532, 776, 821, 829, 1017, 1133, 1241 ; and the pp. *forpyned* only in Prol. 205, A 1453, L. 2428, and R. R. 365. And when we observe that the translator of Fragment A (l. 199), in speaking of false pleaders, expresses *par lor faveles* by 'with hir termes and hir domes,' we can hardly help being reminded of Prol. 323 :—'In termes had he caas and domes alle.'

If we are to reject Fragment A as spurious, we can only conclude that, although fragments of three independent English versions of Le Roman de la Rose have come down to us, not any one of these constitutes any part of the version which Chaucer is known to have made. This is surely somewhat improbable ; if true, it is a case of most exceptional ill luck. If, on the other hand, one of them can be accepted, it must obviously be that which occupies the foremost and the likeliest place, viz. Fragment A.

[1] To the best of my belief this list is correct : achatour, alderman, amblere, anlas, apyked, arrerage, astored, bismotered, blankmanger, bracer, breem, ceruce, chaunterie, cherubin, drogges, dyke, *vb.*, envyned, fithel, flex, floytynge, foot-mantel, forster, fraternitee, fyr-reed, galingale, gauded, ginglen, gipser, goliardeis, grys, *sb.*, haberdasher, harneised, hindreste, knarre, lazar, licentiat, lipsed, lode-menage, love-knotte, luce, medlee, mercenarie, mormal, mortreux, mottelee, nighter-tale, not-heed, outrydere, palmers, parisshens, parvys, pilwebeer, poraille, poudre-marchant, pricasour, pultrye, rote, *sb.* (viol), rouncy, sawce-fleem, scoleye, semicope, sendal, shirreve, snewed, sopin-wyn, stemed, stepe, tabard, taffata, tapicer, trussed, tuft, tukked, undergrowe, vavassour, vernicle, wastel-breed, webbe (weaver), werte, whelkes, y-chaped, yeddinges, yeld-halle, yelding, *sb.*

# APPENDIX

—✦—

## I. List of Chaucer's Works.

The following list is arranged, *conjecturally*, in chronological order. On most points, scholars are agreed.

Of the poems marked (*a*) there seem to have been *two* editions, (*a*) being the earlier. M. P. = Minor Poems (as in the Student's Chaucer).

    Origines upon the Magdaleyne ; *lost.* (See L. G. W., A 418.)

    Book of the Leoun ; *lost.* (See C. T., I 1087.)

    (*a*) Ceys and Alcioun. (Cf. C. T., B 57 ; Bk. Du. 62.)

    Romaunt of the Rose, ll. 1–1705 ; *rest lost.*

    Chaucer's A. B. C. ; M. P. I.

1369. Book of the Duchesse ; M. P. III.

    (*a*) Lyf of St. Cecile. (L. G. W., B 426 ; C. T., G 1.)

    (*a*) Monkes Tale (parts of) ; *except* B 3565–3652.

ab. 1372–3. (*a*) Clerkes Tale ; *except* E 995–1008, and the Envoy.

    Complaint unto Pity ; M. P. II.

    Complaint to his Lady ; M. P. VI.

    (*a*) Translation of the Teseide ; *scraps preserved.*

    Anelida and Arcite (10 stt. *from the* Teseide) ; M. P. VII.

    (*a*) The Tale of Melibeus.

    (*a*) The Persones Tale.

    (*a*) Of the Wrecched Engendring of Mankinde. (L. G. W., A 414 ; cf. C. T., B 99–121, 421–7, 771–7, 925–31, 1132–8.)

    (*a*) Man of Lawes Tale ; *afterwards amplified.*

1377–81. Translation of Boethius.

    The Former Age (*from* Boethius) ; M. P. IX.

    Fortune (*hints from* Boethius) ; M. P. X.

1379 ?. Complaint of Mars ; M. P. IV.

1379–83. Troilus and Criseyde (3 stt. *from the* Teseide).
  Words to Adam (*concerning* Boethius *and* Troilus) ; M. P.
  VIII.

1380–96 ?. Merciless Beautè ; M. P. XI.
  Balade to Rosemounde ; M. P. XII.
  Against Women Unconstaunt ; M. P. XXI.
  Lak of Stedfastnesse ; M. P. XV.
  Gentilesse ; M. P. XIV.
  Truth ; M. P. XIII.
  (*a*) Complaint to his Purse ; M. P. XIX.
  Proverbs ; M. P. XX.
  Womanly Noblesse ; M. P. XXIV.

1382. Parlement of Foules (16 stt. *from the* Teseide) ; M. P. V.

1383–4. Hous of Fame.

1385–6. Legend of Good Women.

1386. Canterbury Tales begun.

1387–8. Central period of the Canterbury Tales.

1389, &c. The Tales continued.

1391. Treatise on the Astrolabe.

1393 ?. Complaint of Venus ; M. P. XVIII.

1393. Lenvoy to Scogan ; M. P. XVI.

1396. Lenvoy to Bukton ; M. P. XVII.

1399. *Envoy to* Complaint to his Purse ; M. P. XIX.

---

*Doubtful Poems.* Complaint d'Amours ; M. P. XXII.
  Complaint to my mortal Foe ; M. P. XXV.
  Complaint to my Lode-Sterre ; M. P. XXVI.

The last two are by the same author, and all three are good examples of *Complaints*, of which Chaucer wrote many. The last two are printed in the six-volume edition, Oxford, 1894. I have also printed (as M. P. XXIII) a short Balade of Complaint ; but it is probably a mere imitation.

## II. List of Authorities for Chaucer's Works.

The meanings of the abbreviations for the various editions and MSS. are given in a separate table below. The works are arranged in the order in which they appear in my larger

edition. In grouping the MSS., I have often borrowed from
the remarks of the editors of the 'Globe' edition.

The number annexed to each poem gives the number of the
lines in it ; thus the *ABC* has 184 lines.

*Romaunt of the Rose* (1705).—G. Th.

MINOR POEMS : I. *ABC* (184).—Group 1 *a*: F. B. Ha.—
Group 1 *b* : P *(two copies)*.—Group 1 *c*: Gg. Sp.—Group
2 *a* : Sion. Bedford.—Group 2 *b* : C. Gl.—Group 2 *c*: L.
Jo. *Also* H.

II. *Complaint unto Pitè* (119).—Group 1 : Sh. Ha.—Group
2 *a* : F. B.—Group 2 *b* : Tn. Ff.—Group 2 *c*: Lt. Trin.
*Also* Ph.

III. *Book of the Duchesse* (1334).—Group 1 *a* : F. B.—Group
1 *b* : Tn.—Group 2 : Th.

IV. *Complaint of Mars* (298).—Group 1 *a* : F.—Group 1 *b*:
Lt. Tn. Th.—Group 2 *a* : P *(two copies)*. Ju. T.—Group
2 *b* : Harl. Ar.

V. *Parlement of Foules* (699).—Group 1 *a*: F. B.—Group
1 *b* : Lt. Tn. D.—Group 2 *a* : Gg. Ff.—Group 2 *b* : Harl.
Trin. O. L. *Also* Ar. Hh. P. Cx.

VI. *Complaint to his Lady* (133).—Sh. Ph. St.

VII. *Anelida* (357).—Group 1 *a* : Harl. T. Ad.—Group 1 *b*:
P. Cx.—Group 2 *a*: H 372, F. B.—Group 2 *b* : Tn. Ff.—
Group 2 *c*: Lt. D. *Also* Ph.

VIII. *Lines to Adam* (7).—T. St.

IX. *The Former Age* (64).—Ii. Hh.

X. *Fortune* (79).—Group 1 : Ii.—Group 2 *a* : A. H.—Group
2 *b*: T.—Group 3 *a*: F. B.—Group 3 *b*: P. Cx. Lan. *Also*
Arch.

XI. *Merciless Beautè* (39).—P.

XII. *To Rosemounde* (24).—R.

XIII. *Truth* (28).—Group 1 *a*: Gg. Ct. E.—Group 1 *b*: At.
Add.—Group 2 *a*: Lan. Cx. F *(two copies)*.—Group 2 *b*:
T *(copy* 1). Harl.—Group 2 *c*: T *(copy* 2).—Group 2 *d* :
Ar. Kk. *Also* P. Arch. Hat. Phil. Corpus.

XIV. *Gentilesse* (21).—Group 1 : T. Harl. A.—Group 2 *a*:
Trinity.—Group 2 *b* : Cx.—Group 2 *c*: Add.—Group 2 *d* :
Ct.—Group 2 *e* : Ha.

XV. *Lak of Stedfastnesse* (28).—Group 1 : T. Harl.—Group

2 *a* : F. Ha. Ct. Add.—Group 2 *b* : Th. Trinity. Ban. *Also* Hat.

XVI. *Envoy to Scogan* (49).—Gg. F. P. Th.

XVII. *Envoy to Bukton* (32).—F. Th. Ju.

XVIII. *Complaint of Venus* (82).—Group 1 : T. A.—Group 2 : F. Tn.—Group 3 : Ju. P (*two copies*).—Group 4 : Ff. Ar.

XIX. *Complaint to his Purse* (26).—Group 1 : F.—Group 2 : Harl. Ff. Add. P. H. *Also* Cx. Ph.

XX. *Proverbs* (8).—F. Ha. Ad. St.

XXI. *Against Women Unconstant* (21).—Group 1 : F.— Group 2 : Ct. Ha. St.

XXII. *Complaint Damours* (91).—Group 1 : Harl.—Group 2 : F. B.

[XXIII. *Balade of Complaint* (21).—Ad.]

XXIV. *Womanly Noblesse* (33).—Addit. 34360.

In the six-volume edition are also given (in vol. iv) : XXV. *Complaint to my Mortal Foe* (32), and XXVI. *Complaint to my Lodesterre* (49) : *both from* Ha.

*Translation of Boethius* (prose).—Group 1 : Camb. Ii. 1. 38 ; Addit. 16165 ; Harl. 2421 ; Cx. ; Bodley 797.—Group 2 : Hengwrt 393 ; Camb. Ii. 3. 21 ; Addit. 10340 ; Salisbury 13 ; Bodley Auct. 3. 5.

*Troilus and Criseyde* (8239).—Phillipps 8252 ; Harl. 3943 ; Harl. 2392 ; Camb. Gg. 4. 27 ; Harl. 4912 ; St. John's (Camb.) ; Rawlinson Poet. 163 ; Harl. 1239 ; Arch. Selden B 24 ; Addit. 12044 ; Durham V. 2. 13 ; Arch. Seld. *supra* 56 ; Digby 181 ; Corp. Chr. Camb. 61 ; Harl. 2280 ; Campsall. *Also* Cx. Th.

*Hous of Fame* (2158).—Group 1 : F. B.—Group 2 : P. Cx. Th.

*Legend of Good Women* (2723).—Group 1 : Gg. P.—Group 2 : F. B. Tn.—Group 3 : Trin. A. Addit. 9832 ; Addit. 12524. *Also* Th.

*Astrolabe* (prose).—Group 1 : Bodley 619.—Group 2 : Camb. Dd. 3. 53 ; Bodl. E Museo 54.—Group 3 : Rawl. D. 913 ; Camb. Dd. 12. 51. *Also* Ashmole 360 and 391 ; Rawl. Misc. 3 ; Addit. 23002 ; Digby 72 ; Corp. Chr. Camb. 424 ; St. John's (Camb.) E. 2 ; Trin. Coll. Cam. R. 15. 18 ; Sloane 261 and 314 ; &c.

*Canterbury Tales* (17385 *and prose*).—E. (Ellesmere); Hn.
(Hengwrt); Cm. (Camb. Gg. 4. 27); Cp. (Corp. Chr. Coll.,
Oxford, 198); Pt. (Petworth); Ln. (Lansdowne 851);
Hl. (Harl. 7334). *In some passages*, Dd. (Camb. Dd.
4. 24); Reg. (Reg. 17 D. xv.); Add. (Addit. 5140); Li.
(Lichfield); Sl. (Sloane 1685); Camb. Ii. 3. 26 and Mm.
2. 5. *There are many more.*

N.B *The Tale of Gamelyn* (902) occurs in Hl. (Harl. 7334);
Harl. (Harl. 1758); Cp. (Corp. Chr. Coll., Oxford); Ln.
(Lansdowne 851); Pt. (Petworth); Rl. (Royal 18 C. ii.);
Sl. (Sloane 1685); Camb. Ii. 3. 26 and Mm. 2. 5. *Also*
Royal 17 D. xv.

---

LIST OF ABBREVIATIONS OF MSS. OF MINOR POEMS.

A. (Ashmole 59, Bodley).—Ad. (Addit. 16165, B. M.).—Add.
(Addit. 22139).—Ar. (Arch. Selden B. 24, Bodley).—Arch.
(Arch. Selden B. 10, Bodley).—At. (Addit. 10340, B. M.).—B.
(Bodley 638).—Ban. (Bannatyne 1568, Glasgow).—Bedford MS.
—C. (Cambridge, Ff. 5. 30).—Corpus (Corp. Chr. Coll., Oxford,
203).—Ct. (Cotton, Cleopatra D. 7, B. M.).—Cx. (Caxton's
editions).—D. (Digby 181, Bodley).—E. (Ellesmere).—F. (Fair-
fax 16, Bodley).—Ff. (Cambridge, Ff. 1. 6).—Gg. (Cambridge,
Gg. 4. 27).—Gl. (Glasgow, Q. 2. 25).—H. (Harleian 2251,
B. M.).—Ha. (Harl. 7578).—Harl. (Harl. 7333).—H 78; *see*
Sh.—H 372 (Harl. 372).—Hat. (Hatton 73, Bodley).—Hh.
(Cambridge, Hh. 4. 12).—Ii. (Cambridge, Ii. 3. 21).—Jo.
(St. John's Coll., Cambridge, G. 21).—Ju. (Julian Notary's
edition).—Kk. (Cambridge, Kk. 1. 5).—L. (Laud 740, Bodley).
—Lan. (Lansdowne 699, B. M.).—Laud (Laud 416, Bodley).—
Lt. (Longleat 258, Marquis of Bath).—O. (St. John's Coll.,
Oxford, 57).—P. (Pepys 2006, Magd. Coll., Cambridge).—Ph.
(Phillipps 9053 = Addit. 34360, B. M.).—Phil. (Phillipps 8299).—
R. (Rawlinson Poet. 163, Bodley).—Sh. (Shirley's MS. Harl. 78,
B. M.)[1].—Sion (Sion College).—Sp. (Speght's edition).—St.
(Stowe's edition).—T. (Trin. Coll. Cam. R. 3. 20).—Th. (Thynne's

---

[1] The symbol Sh. was chosen only for convenience. Shirley's MSS.
are Harl. 78, 2251, and 7333, Ashmole 59, Trin. Coll. Cam. R. 3. 20,
Addit. 16165, and the MS. in Sion College.

edition, 1532).—Tn. (Tanner 346, Bodley).—Trin. (Trin. Coll. Cam. R. 3. 19).—Trinity (Trin. Coll. Cam. R. 14. 51).

### III. CHRONOLOGICAL LIST

of all works associated with Chaucer, in the order of their publication.

\*\*\* This list is arranged solely according to the order in which the Works *first* appeared. The *Genuine* Works have their titles printed *in italics*. By *Canterbury Tales* (1) is meant *first* appearance of the Tales; by *Canterbury Tales* (2) their *second* appearance; and so on. Each piece is only counted *once*; thus the piece succeeding no. 11 is really no. 1, appearing for the second time.

#### EDITIONS BEFORE 1532.

1. Ab. 1477-8. *Canterbury Tales* (1). By Caxton.
2.   ,,    *Parlement of Foules* (1). By Caxton.
3.   ,,    Scogan's Poem, containing *Gentilesse* (1). Same vol.
4.   ,,    *Truth* (1). Same vol.
5.   ,,    *Fortune* (1). Same vol.
6.   ,,    *Envoy to Scogan* (1). Same vol.
7.   ,,    *Anelida* (1). By Caxton.
8.   ,,    *To his empty Purse* (1). Same vol.
9.   ,,    Sayings (1). Same vol.
10. Before 1479. *Boethius* (1). By Caxton.
11. 1483. *Troilus* (1). By Caxton.
    ,,    *Canterbury Tales* (2). By Caxton. See 1.
12.   ,,    *Hous of Fame* (1).
    Ab. 1493. *Canterbury Tales* (3). By Pynson. See 1.
    1498. *Canterbury Tales* (4). By Wynkyn de Worde. See 1.
13. 1499-1502. *Complaint of Mars* (1). By Julian Notary.
14.   ,,    *Complaint of Venus* (1). Same vol.
15.   ,,    *Envoy to Bukton* (1). Same vol.
    1517. *Troilus* (2). By Wynkyn de Worde. See 11.
    1526. *Canterbury Tales* (5). By Pynson. See 1.
    ,,    *Hous of Fame* (2). See 12.
    ,,    *Parlement of Foules* (2). See 2.

16. 1526. La Belle Dame sans Merci (1).   (By Sir R. Ros.) [1]
17.   ,,    Lamentation of Mary Magdaleyne (1).
      ,,    [Moral Proverbs, &c. ; not in later prints.] [2]
      ,,    *Troilus* (3).   See 11.
      1530. *Parlement of Foules* (3).   By Wynkyn de Worde.
            See 2.


EDITION BY W. THYNNE : 1532.

\*\*\* The three first articles were inserted at the end of the
Table of Contents.

18. Eight goodly Questions.
19. { To the Kynges most Noble Grace ;
     { and To the Knights of the Garter.   (By Hoccleve.)
     Sayings (2).   See 9.
     *Canterbury Tales* (6).   See 1.
20. Romaunt of the Rose : *A.* (genuine) ; B. C. (not by Ch.).
    *Troilus* (4).   See 11.
21. Testament of Cresseid.   (By Henryson.)
22. *Legend of Good Women.*
23. A Goodly Balade ('Moder of norture').
    *Boethius* (2).   See 10.
24. *Book of the Duchesse.*
    *Envoy to Bukton* (2).   See 15.
    *Parlement of Foules* (4).   See 2.
25. The Flour of Curtesye.   (By Lydgate.)
26. *Complaint unto Pite.*
    La Belle Dame (2).   (By Sir R. Ros.)   See 16.
    *Anelida* (2).   See 7.
27. The Assembly of Ladies.


[1] Attributed by Pynson to 'Geffray Chaucer,' who (he says) translated it from the French.   See Ames.

[2] Ames gives the contents of the volume, mentioning the Parlement
of Foules, La Belle Dame sauns mercy, Complaint against Fortune,
Certayne Morall Prouerbes of Chaucer, Complaint of Mary Magdaleyne, Letter of Dido, Prouerbes of Lydgate.   But the 'Morall
Prouerbes' had previously been printed by Caxton in 1478, who
expressly says that they were translated from the French by Earl
Rivers.

28. *Conclusions of the Astrolabe.*
29. Complaint of the Black Knight. (By Lydgate.)
30. A Praise of Women.
    *Hous of Fame* (3). See **12**.
31. The Testament of Love. (By T. Usk.)
    The Lamentation of Mary Magdaleyne (2). See **17**.
32. The Remedy of Love.
    *Complaint of Mars* (2). See **13**.
    *Complaint of Venus* (2). See **14**.
33. Letter of Cupid. (By Hoccleve.)
34, 35. Balade in Commendation of our Lady. (By Lydgate.)[1]
36. Praise of Peace. (By Gower.)
37. The Cuckoo and the Nightingale. (By Clanvowe.)
38. Balade : Envoy to Alison.
    Poem quoting *Gentilesse* (2). (By H. Scogan.) See **3**.
39. *Lak of Stedfastnesse.*
    *Truth* (2). See **4**.
    *Fortune* (2). See **5**.
    *Envoy to Scogan* (2). See **6**.
40. Two Stanzas : 'Go forth, King.' (By Lydgate.)
    *To his empty Purse* (2). See **8**.
41. Balade of good Counsel. (By Lydgate.)
    [Epitaphium Galfridi Chaucer.]

W. Thynne's Second Edition : 1542.

Contents the same as in ed. 1532 ; but at the end of the Canterbury Tales was added—
42. The Plowman's Tale.

Undated Edition : about 1550.

Contents the same as in ed. 1542 ; but the Plowman's Tale is made to precede the Parson's Tale.

Edition by John Stowe : 1561. Part I.

Contents as in ed. 1550; but after Gower's ' Praise of Peace ' were inserted—
43. A Saying of Dan John. (By Lydgate.)

---

[1] Two perfectly distinct pieces ; but both are by Lydgate (p. 103).

M

**44.** Yet of the same. (By Lydgate.)
**45.** Balade de bon conseil. (By Lydgate.)
Also after No. **41** was inserted—
    **46.** A Balade in Praise of Chaucer.

## Edition by John Stowe in 1561. Part II.

At the top of fol. cccxl is the following remark :—

¶ Here foloweth certaine woorkes of Geffray Chauser, whiche hath not heretofore been printed, and are gathered and added to this booke by Ihon Stowe.

    *Gentilesse* (3). See **3** and the line below **38**.
**47.** *Proverbs.*
**48.** *A balade whiche Chaucer made against Women Un-constaunt.*
**49.** Beware of Doubleness. (By Lydgate.)
**50.** The Craft of Lovers.
**51.** A Balade. Begins—'Of their nature they greatly them
      delite.' (Quotes No. **60**.)
**52.** The .x. Commaundementes of Loue.
**53.** The .ix. Ladies worthie.
**54.** [Virelai ; no title.] Begins—'Alone walkyng.'
**55.** A Ballade. Begins—'In the season of Feuerere when it
      was full colde.'
**56.** A Ballade. Begins—'O Mercifull and o merciable.'
**57.** The Judgement of Paris.
**58.** A balade pleasaunte.
**59.** An other Balade. Begins—'O Mossie Quince.'
**60.** A Balade, warnyng men to beware of deceitfull women.
      (By Lydgate).
**61.** *Complaint to his Lady.*
**62.** A balade (on the value of chastity.)
**63.** The Court of Love.
**64.** *Lines to Adam Scrivener.*
    [Epitaphium Galfridi Chaucer. In Latin.]
    [The Siege of Thebes. (By Lydgate.)]

## Additions by Speght in 1598.

**65.** The Isle of Ladies ; or, Chaucer's Dream.

66. A Ballad. (Perhaps by Lydgate.)
67. The Flower and the Leaf.

ADDITIONS BY SPEGHT IN 1602.

68. *Chaucer's ABC.*
69. Jack Upland.

ADDITIONS BY URRY IN 1721.

70. The Tale of Gamelyn.
71. The Mery Adventure of the Pardonere and Tapstere; and the Tale of Beryn [1].

APPEARED IN PERCY'S 'RELIQUES' IN 1765.

72. *Merciless Beautè.*

APPEARED IN LEYDEN'S EDITION OF THE COMPLAINT OF SCOTLAND, 1801.

73. Orison to the Virgin. (By Hoccleve.) (1).

ADDITIONS BY BELL IN 1857.

74. Two stanzas by Lydgate; subjoined to Chaucer's Proverbs.
   Orison to the Virgin. (By Hoccleve.) (2).

ADDITIONS BY MORRIS IN 1866.

75. Prosperity. (By John Walton.)
76. *The Former Age.*
77. Leaultè vault Richesse.

ADDITIONS IN SKEAT'S EDITION (1894).

78. *Balade to Rosemounde.*
79. An Amorous Complaint; or Complaint Damours. (Possibly genuine.)
80. Ballade of Complaint. (An imitation.)
81. *Womanly Noblesse.*
82. Complaint to my Mortal Foe.
83. Complaint to my Lode-sterre.
[Nos. 82 and 83 are by the same author, and may be genuine.|

---

[1] Really only *one* piece. 'The Mery Adventure' forms the Prologue to the Tale of Beryn.

M 2

IV. List of Authors connected with 'Chaucer's Works.'

1. Geoffrey Chaucer. Nos. 1, 2, 3 (part), 4, 5, 6, 7, 8, 10, 11, 12, 13, 14, 15, 20 (part), 22, 24, 26, 28, 39, 47, 48 (?), 61, 64, 69, 72, 75, 78, 79 (?), 81, 82 (?), 83 (?).
2. John Gower. No. 36.
3. Thomas Usk. No. 31.
4. Thomas Hoccleve. Nos. 19, 33, 73.
5. (Sir Thomas?) Clanvowe. No. 37.
6. Henry Scogan. No. 3 (quoting 3 stt. by Chaucer).
7. John Lydgate. Nos. 23 (?), 25, 29, 30 (?), 34, 35, 40, 41, 43, 44, 45, 49, 56 (part), 60, 66 (?), 74. And *The Siege of Thebes*.
8. John Walton. No. 76.
9. Sir Richard Ros. No. 16.
10. Robert Henrysoun. No. 21.

The following are anonymous, yet quite distinct from Chaucer and from each other.

11. Author of 'Gamelyn.' No. 70.
12. Author of 'The Ploughman's Crede.' No. 42.
13. The author of Iack Upland. No. 68.
14. A Lady. Nos. 27, 67.
15. A Nun (?). No. 17.
16. Translator of Rom. Rose (B). No. 20.
17. Translator of Rom. Rose (C). No. 20.
18. The author of The Isle of Ladies. No. 65.
19. The author of The Tale of Beryn. No. 71.
20. The author of The Court of Love. No. 63.

The following pieces are by unknown authors, apparently distinct from any of the above. Many of them are clearly distinct from others in the set; but it is not worth while to particularise them. Nos. 9, 18, 32, 38, 46, 50, 51, 52, 53, 54, 55, 56 (part), 57, 58, 59, 62, 77, 80.

It thus appears that, of the above 83 pieces, *at least fifty* are not by Chaucer; whilst the number of authors which they represent is *more than twenty*.

# INDEX